**HOW CHRISTIANS CAN BECOME MORE THAN
CONQUERORS THROUGH SUFFERING**

# DAVID WILKERSON

Triumph Through Tragedy

World Challenge Publications
P.O. Box 260
Lindale, TX 75771

ISBN 0-9712187-0-6

Compiled and edited by Carol B. Patterson

# TABLE OF CONTENTS

## DISCLAIMER

David Wilkerson and his family will receive no money from the sale of this book. Any profits after printing and shipping costs will go directly to the outreaches of World Challenge, especially to addicted mothers and their children.

This book contains testimonies shared with Pastor David Wilkerson by people on his international mailing list. Although the testimonies are true, all names have been changed in order to preserve the privacy of the parties involved.

David Wilkerson has experienced countless challenges and victories throughout his ministry. He has shared some of these struggles publicly, and now he presents the testimonies of others who have endured many trials.

C.S. Lewis, the respected scholar and writer, said, "God, who foresaw your tribulation, has specially armed you to go through it, not without pain but without stain."

Many Christians focus on feeling good and pursuing happiness, but when adverse circumstances interrupt or invade their pursuit, they are forced to make choices. The people you will meet in this book chose to turn to God for answers, and as they sought the Father, He revealed Himself and His nature. You will be amazed at the depth of intimacy with the Father that many gained as they walked through tragedy and hardship.

As you read how these believers triumphed through Jesus Christ, you will be blessed and inspired in your walk with Him. Some have lost children, some have faced cancer and been miraculously healed, others have been abandoned or faced other hardships. The common thread through all their testimonies is the faithful presence and grace of God in their lives, even as they faced their human frailties and questioned Him.

# PART ONE

# MIRACLE HEALINGS

## TERMINAL — The Word I Most Feared

For years I had worked hard and traveled a lot in my job as a sales representative for a large Christian book publisher, and in 1988 I was at the peak of my career. The national sales manager let me know that my territory had risen from the *bottom* to the *top* in sales and total dollar volume of product shipped, and I was elated to hear that all my efforts had paid off.

The day following this good news, I was meeting with my teenage daughter, Emma, who had been undergoing extensive treatment for drug abuse. When Emma saw me, she asked what was wrong with my jaw. "It looks all swollen, Dad." I looked in a mirror and was shocked to see a large, swollen mass around my jaw and neck, something I hadn't noticed before.

I have diabetes, so I immediately went to see my endocrinologist. He thought I might have an infected gland, a cystic growth, or possibly a tumor of some kind. He referred me to a head and neck specialist who found a tumor in the parotid gland (the largest of the three pairs of salivary glands). He assured me that 90 percent of these tumors are benign, and after surgery and a short recovery time, I would be able to get back to work.

The operation was supposed to last only about two hours and my wife patiently waited and waited as hour after hour passed. After six hours, however, she went looking for someone who could tell her what was going on. Finally the surgeon appeared and told her that the tumor had been large and involved, but he was 95 percent certain that he had been able to remove it all and I'd be okay. She told him she'd feel much better after they got the pathologist's report and that last five percent could be resolved in his mind.

The day after my operation, the surgeon stepped into my room wearing a puzzled look on his face. My wife was sitting by my bed and noticed his strange expression right away. He quickly explained that the frozen section of the tumor was being sent to a second pathology lab for another opinion. Audrey is short in stature, but she reared up on her small frame, looked the surgeon in the eye, and asked what was going on. Was the tumor malignant or benign? What could be so complicated about that? The surgeon evaded the question, and mumbled something almost unintelligible about it being the type of tumor the hospital pathologist wasn't confident to make a call on.

The frozen section was sent to a major cancer center and the pathology report came back that the tumor was not only malignant, but it was the kind that could recur within a year or two. Thus began a lengthy period of radiation treatments, along with hyperthermia treatments directly to the area where the tumor had been removed. The combination of the treatments made me very sick with mouth sores and dead taste buds. I survived mostly on milk shakes and Popsicles since I couldn't eat much of anything.

After I got through the treatments, life returned to a form of normalcy and I began to eat and sleep better. I had no energy whatsoever, however, so I just lay around the house and either watched television or slept. After about a year or so of this "lifestyle," I received a call from my sister in another state who told me our mother was acting strange and she needed me to fly home and help her. It turned out Mom had a malignant brain tumor and she had only a short time to live. I helped my sister take care of Mom's affairs, and then I returned to my home and waited.

In the meantime, I was experiencing some disturbing symptoms in the area of my jaw and neck where my tumor had been removed. A scan revealed that the tumor was back and it was suggested that I have a massive portion of my face removed to get it all out. Before we could properly assess this, my mother died and I had to put my attention to that.

After Mom's funeral, we told my surgeon we wanted a second opinion and he referred us back to the big cancer center a few hours from where we lived. The "top head and neck man in America" was there and we wanted the best possible advice. His evaluation was short and blunt: The tumor was indeed back and it had spread to the lymphatic system, the nervous system, and would eventually invade the brain. He said that no surgery would stop the growth of the tumor nor was there any known treatment available. In other words, I was TERMINAL—the word I most feared to hear.

Despair overwhelmed me and I felt betrayed, hopeless, and deeply depressed. My life passed before me and I felt the weight of disappointment, loneliness, and helplessness push me into the dark hole of meaninglessness. I knew that I could avoid further agony with just one massive dose of insulin—so simple and clean. The desire to end it all and "check out" early by my own hand occurred several times, but the grace of God sustained me. He kept providing a glimmer of hope from heaven that prevented me from doing harm to myself.

Then it happened! My Sunday school class asked to pray for me and before I knew it, an outpouring of love, encouragement, and support nearly bowled me over. A fresh, warm sense of hope and peace enveloped Audrey and me as our church not only prayed for us but surrounded us with love, care, and compassion. It was breathtaking! I never really thought that a miraculous healing could take place in my body and I hadn't prayed for it. I was just trying to prepare for death peacefully, and hoped the pain would not be too severe. Ah, but our class wanted more than that—they wanted to have a prayer and healing service for us. This seemed too far out, because we were in a Baptist church and we *didn't do* healing services. Audrey and I finally consented to let the class pray over me for healing, and somebody even anointed me with oil.

I didn't really feel much going on, to be absolutely truthful. The day after the prayer, I was back in my depression and self-pity, knowing that my days on earth were getting shorter. I even called my family together and made sure my will was updated.

Several months passed and I actually began to feel better. The cards and letters and phone calls kept showing the love of God's people as they prayed. They had hope that I would get better even though my cynical spirit would not allow me to grasp that flame of hope. However, I did notice that I wasn't dying!

I decided to call my doctor and see if he would order another scan to see if anything was changing. He consented and the results were so startling that he ordered more tests to confirm the scan. The mass had disappeared! All the medical experts were left scratching their heads and wondering what had happened. Then it struck me that GOD had actually done something to the tumor mass in my body because the people of God had prayed for me. GOD had actually answered their prayers!

Now I know for sure that God really does answer the prayers of those who truly believe in His power to heal when all else seems hopeless and meaningless. Praise God for all those who kept praying for me when I didn't believe that the God of all creation could or would heal me and take away my cancer!

I don't understand why I am living today since I have seen so many of my loved ones, friends and acquaintances leave this life because of cancer. I just know that as long as the Lord Jesus Christ gives me breath, I will trust Him, lean on Him completely, and praise Him for His sustaining grace and healing mercies. Hallelujah!

## My Glory and the Lifter of My Head

A tumor had eaten away the first and second vertebrae in my neck and it broke—that's right, my neck broke! I had four operations in the span of a week and a half, performed by two surgeons—one was a trained surgeon and the other was God. I was literally rebuilt with metal plates, cement, wire, nuts, bolts and screws, along with my own bone to stabilize my neck. I stayed in the hospital more than a month and was fitted with a "halo," a metal apparatus to keep everything in place. I wore the halo for over five months, and during that time I was fed a liquid diet through a tube in my nose that went into my stomach. After I got out of the halo, I wore a hard collar for four more months. This was such a humbling experience.

During this ordeal, God showed my husband, Ben, and me verses in the Bible that helped us so much.

"Fear thou not; for I am with thee: be not dismayed;

11

for I am thy God: I will strengthen thee; yea, I will help thee; yea, I will uphold thee with the right hand of my righteousness." (Isaiah 41:10)

I will admit that I was depressed at times, but this verse reassured me. My husband was such a help to me, reading the Bible daily and sharing words the Lord had given to him. I was lifted up and I knew God was with me all the way.

For four years I was limited in what I could do, but I enjoyed the wonders of our Father. You learn to appreciate the little things. At the end of four years, I had another scan done and again a large tumor was found. The doctor told me I definitely needed radiation. In consultation with a specialist in the field, I was told that just regular, normal radiation would not work; I needed a more precise type. Since there were only two places in the U.S. that had these particular radiation machines, I had to choose where we would go. We chose the hospital on the east coast, made an appointment, and drove to it.

When we met the doctor who was to treat me, he reviewed the films and reports that we had hand-carried to him. When I told him I was able to walk, talk, and move my neck, he was amazed. He said he really couldn't understand how I was even alive, much less mobile. He thought that the way my neck had broken should have killed me instantly, but there I was, walking and talking with him. He explained the massive doses of radiation that I would be receiving over the next eight weeks, five days a week. He further explained that they needed at least three centimeters between the tumor and my spinal cord in order to administer the treatment, and he had to be sure I still had that space. If not, I would have to have surgery again. On top of this, there was one more problem: It would be at least four months before I could get into the program.

The doctor wanted to review all the biopsy slides, all scans, x-rays, and reports for the last four years to the present, so Ben and I drove home, got all the records together, and sent them to him. We called our pastor and explained what was going on, then we settled in to wait to hear from the doctor. We didn't have any idea it would take so long for him to get back to us, but we now realize things were moving along according to God's timetable and not ours.

When we heard from the doctor after several weeks, it was not good news. He said he and another specialist had reviewed all my tests and they agreed that I needed to get started on radiation right away. He told me the bone in my neck had been eaten away by the tumor and the metal plate that had been placed in there was just floating around. He expressed amazement that I could hold my head up, and then he told me to be sure to wear the hard collar I had from my first surgery. They arranged to start my radiation treatments right before Christmas.

Ben and I called the pastor and told him what the doctor had said. I will admit I was pretty nervous, but that night a friend called and gave us a Bible verse the Lord had impressed upon her:

"But thou, O Lord, art a shield for me; my glory, and the lifter up of mine head." (Psalm 3:3)

This verse confirmed to Ben and me who was *really* holding up my head!

The doctor called again and asked me to have a myelogram done and the results sent to him immediately so he could see if the space he needed for the radiation was present. My neurosurgeon did the myelogram himself and he discovered something unusual: A mass was growing behind where the metal plate and bone had been. At first that sounded like bad news, but it was actually very good.

My films were sent to the doctor on the east coast on a Friday. On the following Wednesday, he called and this is exactly what he said: *"I have reviewed your case with several radiologists and the bottom line is that we do not see any progression of your tumor...Things look actually quite stable. The fusion, nothing has slipped, no bone slipped and no further erosion, which is great. It is a giant cell tumor and it is possible you may need radiation in the future. Now a couple of my neurosurgeons have actually wanted to look at this case very carefully and I am actually reviewing it with the spinal neurosurgeon here. There is no immediate need for radiation."*

A couple of days later the doctor called again and this is what he said, *"Bottom line is, I don't believe you need treatment at this time. No evidence that tumor is growing. Have been over the films very carefully with neurosurgeons and no change; everything looks quite stable."*

Ben and I were so excited that God had answered our prayers. We realize that the neurosurgeons who wanted to go over my case had no idea what had happened, but we know—and we have proof! God intervened! Many prayer groups were praying for me and He answered prayer. I am so very thankful to all the loving people who prayed and I especially thank our pastor for his kindness and understanding.

During my whole ordeal I had a strong, loving husband who stood by me and gave me strength. With God's help, we have both come through this crisis stronger, knowing that He works miracles—and I am one of them.

## Taking Back What Satan Tried to Steal

In 1995 my daughter, Luci, was diagnosed with leukemia exactly 26 years after my husband, her father, died from leukemia. The doctors gave her one month to live unless she received immediate, extreme treatment, so she flew to San Francisco where she could get the care she needed.

Two weeks before her diagnosis, God had impressed Luci's spirit with Mark 5:34: "Daughter, your faith has made you whole." She had no idea why this Scripture was made so real to her, but she stored it in her mind.

Luci endured very intense treatments over the next six months, with three lengthy hospital stays. She and her husband had to go almost 300 miles from their home for these treatments and this was difficult, as they were separated from their work and children. But they held on to the Scriptures God had given them.

Luci's condition was exceptionally precarious at times. At one point her platelets got so low that she was not allowed to even move without a nurse present, and extreme precautions were taken to keep her from bleeding to death. Another time she contracted an infection that could have taken her life. Throughout this whole ordeal, people all over the world were praying for her—many individuals, churches, and prayer groups. When she got the dangerous infection, I called several groups for special prayer and within 24 hours the infection was gone—a complete miracle of God!

Early in my daughter's first treatment, God gave me the Scripture John 11:4: "This sickness is not unto death, but for the glory of God, that the Son of Man may be glorified through it." I stood on this Scripture through those long six months. Luci was in the hospital a total of 102 days, and went through intense chemotherapy and a peripheral stem cell transplant. I kept her three children a total of nine weeks during her illness (they were 11, 7 and 3 at the time). It was hard on the children, especially the three-year-old, who couldn't understand why she couldn't be with her mommy. God gave us all strength and the daily guidance we needed to get through this difficult time. It is impossible to describe the strength of the Holy Spirit that we experienced—but believe me, He held us steady during the ups and downs that we faced each day.

Luci made it through; it has now been six years since she was first diagnosed with leukemia and there has been no recurrence. The enemy wasn't finished attacking Luci, though. A friend had a setback and died from leukemia a couple of years ago. She had been in treatment at the same time Luci had, and this triggered a bout with terrible fear. For 18 months Luci waged a day-by-day struggle to overcome the fear that gripped her. She sought the Word of God and He was faithful to give her many promises, which she stood on. God also sent people to her at strategic times with words of encouragement. Truly the enemy was a liar! During that time, all her blood tests remained normal. Glory to God.

We are all so thankful for God's strength, help, guidance, and grace during our time of extreme testing. God is faithful! We didn't know if Luci would live or die, but we did know that God would stand by us, regardless of what happened. When He gave us Scriptures, we stood on them and believed Him for a miracle! Thank God! I have been through many difficult times in my life and God has never failed me. He has ministered to me in so many ways, at so many times, and I love Him for it.

## It's Too Dangerous to Operate — And Without Surgery You May Die!

For at least 17 years, I suffered strange feelings in my head—sometimes it was pressure, at other times I had distorted vision, or saw lights dancing in my eyes. And most terrible of all were the headaches. During those years I went to many doctors and was told that my condition was probably due to stress or hypertension. Then there were those not so subtle suggestions that it was "all in my head"—which, of course, it was! I went to a psychiatrist and to a stress clinic for therapy, but got no relief. Often I was made to feel like a hypochondriac, until I decided, NO MORE DOCTORS! I turned to Jesus and cried out to Him, because He alone knew what was wrong with me *and He was the only One who could help me.*

In spite of severe headaches, I tried to maintain a normal life. The light and pain in my eyes occurred frequently and at times I would go temporarily blind. I even passed out a couple of times, once on an airplane. I was told that I either had a heart problem or an inner ear imbalance. My husband and I just kept praying and seeking the Lord—that's all we knew to do.

A couple of days after returning home from a wonderful vacation with our daughter and her family, I suffered an episode that changed the course of our lives forever. My husband, Tom, was driving us home after shopping when my head went totally numb. All I could see was white and I thought surely I was dying. I screamed and scared poor Tom half to death. The feeling quickly returned to my head, but I felt weak and tired. Tom wanted to take me to the local emergency hospital, but I just wanted to go home and rest. I thought I would be all right—and I didn't want to go to another doctor!

Ten days later, I was still feeling awful, so I broke down and went to Dr. Anderson. He took blood tests and said that if I had any further problems I should call him. Two days later I awoke with such a terrible headache that I called him, but it was his day off. Tom called one of our daughters, Becky, who is a nurse, and she insisted that I go in to see our son-in-law, Allen, a doctor. Allen was aware of many of the problems and suffering I had endured and he said he felt it was time to really check it out. He ordered an MRI (magnetic resonance imaging) of my head and later that afternoon he and Becky stopped by to see us. As soon as they walked in the door, I knew they had found something. Yes, they certainly had!

The MRI showed that I had a large tumor, a meningioma, at the top of my head, lying like a pancake between the brain and the skull. It measured 5" x 4" and it was ¹/₂" thick. It had already done a lot of damage—now we understood all the symptoms I had suffered for so long. There was some good news along with the bad; this type of tumor is very slow growing and there is only about a one percent chance of malignancy. However, if left to grow, it could eventually cover the entire inside of my skull. The doctor felt I should have it removed, giving me hope of feeling better than I had felt for years.

This type of news has a tremendous, dramatic impact on one's life. Tom and I had to cancel our plans for a cruise with special friends that we had looked forward to. I felt so bad, even guilty, about this, because we had talked them into making the trip. In spite of the disappointment, however, we had to face the fact that our lives were totally changed.

I was sent to a neurologist immediately and my long journey of emotional and physical challenges began. He put me on medication to prevent a stroke or seizure but it made me so dizzy that I was almost incapacitated. More tests followed and I became so sick that I spent my days just lying around, unable to perform even the simplest tasks. I became totally dependent on others.

This ordeal was very debilitating and I went through a time of terrible depression. We called everyone we knew that would pray and believe God for a miracle. A dear friend suggested that I have the elders of the church lay hands on me and pray in obedience to the Word of God (James 5:14,15). "Is anyone sick among you? Let him call for the elders of the church and let them pray over him, anointing him with oil in the name of the Lord; and the prayer offered in faith will restore the one who is sick, and the Lord will raise him up, and if he has committed sins, they will be forgiven him." My faith for a miracle soared at that time. Not only did I have that special prayer by my pastor and friends at church, but I started hearing of many from other churches, friends, and family who were praying. I began to *know* that God would give me the miracle touch I needed.

A second neurologist, a specialist in the type of tumor I had, was totally honest with us and explained that my situation was so dangerous that he did not recommend surgery. If I didn't have surgery, the tumor would continue to grow and cover my head, yet we were told that surgery was not recommended. Tom and I went home totally distraught! We learned again that man is so limited, and we knew that only the power of God could intervene for us.

We got several varying reports from doctors during the next weeks. We would be told one thing that sparked hope only to discover that it was not true. During this time our emotions were like a yo-yo—up with hope, then down with despair! We were learning quickly to focus on God's Word and stand on it. God said, "I am the Lord that healeth Thee," and our confidence was in Him. We could not rely on the varied reports and physical symptoms, so we chose to believe His promises. I knew that except for a miracle from the Lord, I didn't have much hope.

I surrendered myself to the Lord, for I knew that my life was in His hands. Whether I lived or died, I knew it was okay, for God does all things well. Tom and I prayed for His will to be done, but there were still times when I wished for death, because I saw no help coming. Then the Lord ministered to me through His Word: "That I may know Him, and the power of His resurrection, and the fellowship of His sufferings, being conformed to His death, if by any means I may attain to the resurrection from the dead." (Phil. 3:10,11) The Lord showed me over and over that He rose to give me LIFE, not death, and He wanted me to have that resurrection power in my life. I wanted to know Him in that intimate way and sought for it. In turn, God touched my heart and I knew He was undertaking for me.

God encouraged us and taught us in many different ways, and He ministered to me on countless levels. The Lord provided exactly what I needed each day and He used His children to encourage and help us. Friends and family helped with the housework, sent flowers, made phone calls, came to visit—and most importantly, they *all* prayed. There were five special ladies in the church who committed themselves to praying for my healing. They gave me constant encouragement and Scripture verses to build my faith. They told me things like, "The battle is not yours, but the Lord's" and "Your life is now hidden with Christ in God." Because of their faithfulness, I constantly knew that my life was in God's hands.

During some of our lowest times, Tom and I received songs from the Lord in the night. We sang many of the old and dear hymns when we couldn't sleep, and one especially stands out: "Victory Ahead!" How faithful God was to us during this time.

After a long wait, we were able to see the chief neurologist to get his opinion. For the first time, we heard a positive response from a doctor, a man with impeccable credentials and experience. He pointed out three options to us: we could do nothing; we could wait for years and then do something; or I could have surgery right away. And he thought if we went ahead with surgery, I had a 90 percent chance for success. Well, that was better news than we had heard in the past. He told us to go home and think about it before making a decision.

That week was filled with turmoil, because we wanted to trust God completely, and yet I was told that there was not much hope without surgery. What should I do? I was reminded that God uses doctors and when He does, it doesn't take away from the fact that *God alone* is the healer. We scheduled surgery, and after the anguish of the struggle in making the decision, I was so happy. We were told to enjoy our holidays with our family and face the surgery afterwards.

During the wait, my support system was wonderful. The prayer was constant and we were sustained and very, very blessed. I felt unworthy and overwhelmed as the cards came, visitors stopped in and brought meals, and flowers arrived. Tom's caring support and protection meant so much to me and together we drew closer to the Lord and each other.

Tom had been experiencing a lot of pain in his back and it was determined that he needed surgery right away—even before my surgery. His recovery was so quick and complete that we could only thank the Lord, the Great Physician. Our children were magnificent during this time and somehow we all weathered the stress and agitation that sometimes arose.

My surgery was long and involved, and the neurologist later told us that he was able to remove only about 75 percent of the deadly growth. Then there was the recovery period, and physical therapy, and all that goes with major surgery. But because of prayer, I had confidence throughout the whole time. I knew it was because of God's faithfulness, His Word, and the guidance of the Holy Spirit that I was brought through this dark time. I was able to totally surrender everything to Him—after all, I had trusted Him with my life!

When I was able to return home, I felt wrapped in the love of Jesus. No matter what I needed, the Lord provided it through my church, friends, and family. I will never be able to fully thank them for the love of Jesus I saw manifested in them. Although I had some problems now and then, every time I went to be checked, nothing was found. Finally a nurse realized that a drug I was on was causing problems.

Several weeks after my surgery, a follow-up scan was done. The doctor could not see anything on the scan, even though he knew he had left some of the tumor in. We knew that our

Great Physician had caused the rest to dry up—the scan was clean!

I believe God gave me the miracle that so many prayed for! I praise the Lord and bless His holy name.

About three months after my surgery, Tom had a heart attack. Here I was, still recovering, and he was concerned about me, but he ended up having more surgery himself. He was pretty well recovered from his back surgery, but this heart attack was very hard on us. Then two weeks after his heart surgery, he became very ill and was rushed to the hospital where he had to have *more* surgery. His gall bladder had to be removed because gangrene had set in. Here we were, both laid up. Then Tom got sick again and this time the diagnosis was pancreatic cancer. Very soon he went home to be with the Lord.

I tell you this to emphasize that through it all, God has been very real. After my husband's death, I really felt forsaken for a time, and at times I thought I couldn't make it. But the wonder of it all is that in all these things I have had the loving, almighty hand of God do miracles and see me through. I am fully recovered and happy to report that there are no lingering effects of my brain tumor—and they still can't find anything! My great joy at the time of writing this is that I am preparing for a missions trip to Asia, so God not only met my needs, He is giving me the desires of my heart.

We have nothing to brag about except Him. All the praise, glory, honor, and worship belong to God the Father and to His precious Son, my Savior.

## You Have a New Heart

I couldn't believe it! I had started the day visiting friends in the hospital and here I was a patient myself.

My blood pressure was extremely high, I had a gurgling

sound in my chest, and I was having difficulty breathing. An IV was dripping something into my arm, an oxygen mask covered my face, and I was hooked up to a heart monitor. I wasn't in much discomfort, but that suddenly changed. Without warning, a sharp pain shot through my chest and they rushed me to the critical care unit.

Soon after I received medication to bring my blood pressure down, everything went black and I passed out. The medication had worked *too well* and my blood pressure went too low. At ceiling height, I saw Jesus sitting on a white throne. With His elbow on the arm of the chair and His chin resting on His hand, He looked down at me and asked, "Well, Ellie, do you want to stay here or come home with Me?"

What a choice! Before I could answer, I saw the faces of my husband, family, and friends flash before me. They were shaking their heads and mouthing, "NO!" Looking back at Jesus, I replied, "I'll stay." He answered, "Okay," and disappeared. The next thing I remember was a nurse faintly saying, "Her pressure is starting back up."

They told me I had congestive heart failure and I spent five days in the hospital. When they sent me home, I was ordered to cut my activities by two-thirds and lose thirty pounds. The doctor wanted me to walk at least a mile a day when I regained my strength.

I was a retreat speaker, a counselor, and co-pastor with my husband, and I did all my own housework. As you can imagine, this new regimen was a major change in lifestyle for me. Church members, family, and friends helped me all they could and showered me with love, prayers, and encouragement. That year was filled with emotional and spiritual experiences that resulted in a greater trust in God and a better self-image.

I was shocked when about a year later, I was back in the hospital suffering a heart attack of a different nature. The day before, I had experienced severe pain in my arm and neck, but after my husband prayed for me, I got some relief. However, we went ahead and made an appointment with my doctor, who was about sixty miles from where we lived. I was astonished when the doctor came out after having done tests and said, "I have made arrangements for you to go directly to the hospital and the care flight helicopter is on its way to take you there."

My husband immediately called some of our close friends for prayer, and they cried out to God for us. When the male nurses were getting me ready for the flight, they bundled me up and gently lifted me onto the gurney. What a pleasant feeling it was to be lifted and carried to the helicopter. As they were carrying me, the Lord spoke to me, "This is the way I want you to let Me carry you. Are you willing to give it all to Me?" I thought about it for a moment, then answered Him, "Yes. Whatever happens, I am at peace with You. If I have to have an operation, that's all right. If I die, that's all right, too. I give it all to You!"

I was too sick to know much about the flight to the hospital, but after we arrived and the doctor there had examined me, he said, "It looks like you are on the verge of a major heart attack."

The next day, my husband called a local Pentecostal pastor and he came to visit; our daughter and several minister friends were there, as well. They all prayed for me just before I was taken in for a heart catheterization. After prayer, the local pastor exclaimed, "It's done!"

When the doctor finished the heart cath, he looked at me and said, "You have a perfectly normal, healthy heart. There isn't a thing wrong with it."

Rather astonished by the news, I asked, "Is there any sign of the damage of a year ago?" and he replied, "No."

"Is there any damage from the attack I had yesterday?" Again, the reply was, "No."

"Well, what about cholesterol in my arteries?" I asked. His reassuring words were, "There's not even a speck! I'm telling you, you have a healthy, normal heart. It's like a new heart!"

Before I had gone for the heart catheterization, all my vital signs were abnormal; however, when I got back in my room, they were all normal. Every time they took my vital signs, the nurses would exclaim, "They're normal!"

When the doctor came to visit me in the evening, my husband excitedly told him, "God has performed a miracle of healing on my wife!" The doctor couldn't argue with that, and he said, "You can't get any better than that or add anything to it."

As the doctor started for the door, I said, "Doctor, I think I'm beginning to comprehend what has happened to me."

"No! You haven't! It will take you months to comprehend it all. You are not the same woman, physically, who was flown in here two days ago." He was animated and thrilled to be able to tell me that. "You can do anything you want to do, go anywhere you wish, and eat anything you want."

My daughter was standing right there and said, "But you don't know my mom's schedule, Doctor."

"Well, start out slowly and within reason." Then he turned and walked out the door.

I was dismissed from the hospital the following day and upon my return home, I resumed all my regular activities, even doing things I couldn't do before. I was able to go hiking with my family without getting exhausted. I have helped my husband shovel snow off our driveway and walkways.

My husband and I went with friends to a famous mountain and climbed the 380 steps up to the top. We all raised our hands and praised the Lord for His healing power. The Bible says that Jesus is the same yesterday, today, and forever (Hebrews 13:8). He healed my heart the same way He healed people in Bible days.

A few months before the Lord healed me, He gave me a promise: "A new heart also will I give you, and a new spirit will I put within you." (Ezekiel 36:26)

I am awed by the change in my spirit. The Lord has given me a deeper understanding of His love and He has also given me a forgiving heart.

The doctor had said to me, "There is not a speck of cholesterol in your veins." After a meeting where I gave my testimony, a nurse came up to me and said, "The Lord must have given you a new circulatory system, because we all, even babies, have *some* cholesterol in our veins."

Because of my testimony, at least six people have been healed of heart problems (and these are just the ones I know about). "But He was wounded for our transgressions, He was bruised for our iniquities: the chastisement of our peace was upon Him; and with His stripes we are healed." (Isaiah 53:5)

## What Can Fear Do to Me?

When my children were small, they would occasionally wake up from a scary dream and cry out for Mom or Dad, screaming and sobbing. The only way I could calm them was to hold them close, reassuring them that everything was fine, Mommy was there. Then we would pray, and as I rocked them back to sleep, I would ask God to come and bring peace to their little hearts. I remember so well the short little breaths they gasped as they snuggled close and fell back to sleep. They knew I would not let anything harm them and that Jesus was watching over them. Every mother treasures these memories.

A couple of years ago, I was the "scared little child" standing in the hallway of a hospital, trying to stifle those same little gasps and sobs. I dreaded the results of a blood test that

I knew would be fine, yet feared would send me back to the hospital.

Three years earlier I had been diagnosed with leukemia, and while enduring some harsh treatment, I had battled fear. In fact, at times I had been petrified with fear! But God ministered to my entire family and brought me through this life-threatening illness with a clean bill of health. God spoke to me through His Word and sent peace that never left me. During my whole ordeal, I never feared death!

That is, not until three years later when I found out that a dear friend had just died. We had been in treatment together and had become "comrades in the fight." Suddenly I feared that I, too, might succumb to the ravages of the disease. Like Peter walking on the water, I saw the waves around me and began to sink rapidly! I cried out in the dark and in my thrashing around, I moved away from the gentle but firm security He had provided for me during the previous years. I went under, again and again, but I had enough equilibrium to fight.

As I sought God for help, the first Scripture reference He brought to my mind was the one He had given me three years prior, Psalm 56:3 and 4: "When I am afraid, I will trust in you. In God whose word I praise, in God I trust; I will not be afraid. What can mortal man do to me...?" The ensuing year was difficult for me. I would just begin to get my fear under control and recognize God's hand in my life when I would get a headache, or my heart would go wild with palpitations. Every time any little sickness would hit me, I would immediately think I had relapsed, and the whirlpool of fear would swirl around me again. Nine times that year I "just had to have" a blood test to make sure I had not relapsed, as I feared. There was a point that my husband thought I might be headed for a nervous breakdown because I was so obsessed with my health. In desperation, I knew I had to find God's arms—and I had to find them fast!

My fear drove me to His Word and God was so faithful, as He always is. A song straight from the Bible became ingrained in my spirit: "I am the Lord that healeth thee, I am the Lord your healer. I sent my Word and healed all your disease, I am the Lord your healer." (From Exodus 15:26) I sang that song over and over and over again until I felt it become a part of me. Gradually I began to rely on His strength and rest in His care, knowing that the promises He had given me throughout that year were true. There were too many that had come to me in too many different ways to be mere coincidence.

I prayed constantly—many days I prayed literally moment by moment, all day long. It was the only way I knew to keep my feet on the ground. Many times I called friends and when I saw friends at church, I asked them to pray for me. This was my lifeline!

I praised often—I learned new songs and sang old ones. I repeated Scriptures of promise and praise to God. I encouraged myself in the Lord and asked others to encourage me and remind me who God was to me. I spoke out loud the attributes of God, His holiness, His faithfulness, His omnipotence, His love, and so forth. I said aloud that Jesus had victory over Satan and his attacks on my life and my emotions. In other words, I verbally gave Jesus control of my life!

Then I had to practice what God brought my way. That was hardest for me, because I had to get it past my brain into my heart. I had to begin believing that God's promises were not just for that day, but were for the rest of my life! I forced myself to *act on the fact* that God's promises were true! Even though I sometimes felt like I was going crazy, I just kept on repeating Scripture verses. And God's Word came through!

In the next year I had 13 blood tests (which I "needed") and I finally had my last one, which I called "my victory CBC." This was more than just a test; it was closure to months of turmoil and fear, the final chapter to the book of testing I endured. I was able to rejoice with that test and know that truly He is God.

Every day I now face the issue of fear, thinking that I might relapse, and the medical people tell me that I'll have some aspect of that for the rest of my life. The difference for me is that now my head is held high and I am no longer slinking around in fear. I daily choose to believe God's promises and rest in them. And I encourage others to do the same.

## Keeping It All Together in the Wilderness

I am a 46-year-old man who had reached the pinnacle of success in a billion-dollar corporation. When new management took over, I tried in vain to fit in to the new regime, but it just wasn't working. I didn't see any way I could stay, so I asked if we could possibly settle on a graceful exit with a good severance package. Only two days later I was asked to leave—for having a bad attitude! And there would be no settlement—just two weeks' vacation pay. Period.

The next seven months were a tremendous test of my marriage and my faith in God. My wife and I have two accomplished children who fill our lives with joy, and by the grace of God the family came through this wilderness intact. The Lord opened up the door for me to start an independent business during this time.

In August of 2000, I suffered a seizure at home and tests showed that I had a large brain tumor. Subsequent surgery and pathology revealed that the tumor was malignant and I was told that the statistics indicated a survival time of a little over two years. I have endured radiation treatments and am currently undergoing chemotherapy. My MRI's are clear and the oncologist tells me I'm doing well—*considering*.

The Lord has led me deep into His Word and I rejected

most of the clichéd verses regarding healing, because I didn't sense Him speaking them into my heart. He led me to Ezekiel 47, which has become the cornerstone of healing for my life. This portion of Scripture (especially verses 7 through 12) speaks about the river that flows from the throne of God and the trees that grow along that river. The trees have leaves of healing and produce a new crop of fruit every month.

I feel that God has given me another chance to live for Him. Even though my wife doesn't like to hear me say this, I have told the Lord that if I do not stay in Him daily, then He can just take me home. Furthermore, I believe that my healing is in those leaves (the Word of God) and this is what keeps the cancer away from me.

Fifteen years ago I was on a drilling rig that collapsed during a hurricane. Several people died and I floated in a capsule for ten hours, tossed around by waves up to 35 feet high. I feared for my life, but God was merciful. In the weeks following my rescue, I made many vows to the Lord, and for seven or eight years I thought I was doing everything He wanted me to. In the last seven or eight years, however, I had been caught up in my career and had become lukewarm in my soul.

There may be several reasons I got cancer. Perhaps my early drug use or even chemicals in the environment contributed to it. I believe with all my heart that Satan uses many unknown corruptions of this world to destroy God's creation. I'll leave the answers with Him; the good news is that what the enemy meant for my destruction, God has turned for my good.

I am happy to share some of the things I've learned over the last few months:

1. When faced with a crisis, you must turn your *entire being* toward His throne.

2. You weep with bitterness, not toward God but toward your

own lukewarm attitude regarding so great a salvation.

3. You must be willing to surrender your life.
4. You learn the truth of what Paul said, "To die is gain."
5. Even though you believe in healing, your faith is put to the test.
6. He has given me compassion:
   a. To visit the sick
   b. To pray for people
   c. To reach out and close the gaps in family relationships.

Finally, Paul tells us that in our suffering, we receive the blessing with which we comfort others. Thank God that every trial provides an opportunity to receive the glory of God into our lives. This enables us to go forth with power and share the greatness of God with a hurting world.

## Whose Report Do We Believe?

I grew up in a Catholic family but started going to a Methodist church when I met my wife. During our growing-up years neither of us drank, used drugs or ran around partying, even though a lot of that was going on during the 60's and 70's. I believe God spared us those troubles in order to bear witness to His grace and mercy, and to illustrate that you don't have to go through really dramatic and "colorful" times in order to have a great testimony.

My wife and I both accepted Jesus as Savior after we were married and our lives seemed perfectly on track until the early 90's when I got my first diagnosis of cancer—at 39 years of age. I was in perfect health and my favorite sport was riding mountain bicycles in the hills around where we lived. I thought I was an invincible Christian, but that feeling came crashing down around me when they found the colon cancer.

I now know that God was clearly speaking to me about my walk with Him. I would sit in church and daydream about everything except Him and the Word. I had lost my true focus and He was sending me a wake-up call. And I listened! I had the necessary surgery and was declared cancer-free.

Three short years later, the cancer returned in a different location. Interestingly, this was a very rare type of cancer, especially for my age group. I was treated with chemotherapy and radiation and, yes, again God was getting my full attention. I vowed to continue working every day, regardless of how I felt or looked, and by His grace I never missed a day of work. Praise the Lord! Going through this experience enabled me to relate to cancer patients in a new way and I wanted to inspire others to look to the Lord for strength and comfort. After I completed this round of treatments, I was declared free of cancer again.

During this time I was playing in a Christian band that went from church to church witnessing to others in the name of Jesus Christ. We saw the hand of God at work in our group and in those we ministered to. The leader of the band wrote awesome, Spirit-inspired songs that drew people to Jesus. Unfortunately, we disbanded because the enemy crept in and destroyed what God had started. How I miss those times of ministry! Even though it was hard work, it was worth all the effort because of God's blessing.

Just one year later, cancer again returned to my life. How I came to hate the word CANCER. However, I had come to know that God is always in control! Once again I told God that if "having cancer helps me reach others, then preserve me with Your grace and mercy, and heal me once again." I went through another round of chemotherapy, again without missing one day of work, and I continued to live a life centered on Christ.

This time the cancer was found in the lymph nodes and the doctor told me it will come back someday. I don't believe that report! I believe Jesus did a complete healing in my body and it is a perfect work. His hand has surely been upon me for a purpose on this earth. It has been almost four years since my last cancer and I am still here by His grace.

I won't suggest that these have not been tough years, because they have, but I am so glad I have had the opportunity to reach others through my compassion, and witness to them in Jesus' name. I wouldn't want to go through cancer again, but I would if I had to in order to help someone from "falling into the fire." As it says in the Book of Jude, we must snatch those from the fire like a burning stick, just as He saved me. I love the last verses in Jude that say He is able to keep us from falling, and He will present us to Himself as perfect and receive us with great joy. This is such an awesome revelation of His great love for us all.

I thank God daily for my walk with Him and I thank Him for my family. For 25 years my wife, Jan, has stood by my side and she has walked through all of this with me. She is a great warrior in God's army and I'm deeply thankful for her. God is so special in our lives and I wish that everyone could experience His great love, mercy and grace, for without that we are nothing.

## A Frenzy of Fear

Victories are wonderful and all people want to have them, but we must remember that many times victory comes through suffering. Trials are involved and there are lessons to be learned. The victory the Lord gave me involved both trials and lessons.

I thought I knew a lot about the Christian life and I was actively trying to do God's will when all of a sudden, everything crashed in on me. My doctor called and asked me to come to the office for a chat. I suspected nothing and was stunned when she told me that the CT scan, which my other physician had ordered, revealed a tumor on my brain. I had had a slight irregularity in my calcium level and both my husband and doctor felt a scan would be helpful to be sure there was no underlying problem. No one thought anything would show up, so when the doctor told me the findings, it was such a jolt that I went into a state of shock. Fear gripped me like I had never experienced and I imagined all kinds of catastrophic things. The Lord, who is gracious and merciful, gave me peace in my soul through the verse, "I sought the Lord, and He heard me, and delivered me from all my fears." But my humanity kept me in a frenzy for several weeks.

No matter how upset I became or what went on in my mind or around me, I knew that Jesus was keeping my soul under His blood and all would be well. Our precious Lord helped us find out about this tumor, which the doctor said had been in the making for possibly 30 years. We wouldn't have known about it but for the providence of God.

Prayers began to go up to the Lord's throne on my behalf and that meant more to me than anything else in the world. My children and husband began interceding for me and my son sent me this verse: "I am the Lord that healeth thee." (Exodus 15:26) I took it as coming directly from the Lord.

Wonderful songs spoke to my soul during this time. "I Know Whom I Have Believed" by D. W. Whittle and "Be Still and Know (That I am God)" by Mrs. Hal Buckner contained powerful messages that ministered to me.

"As for God, His way is perfect." (Psalm 18:30) Some saints were able to sing while in prison; some walked the martyr's trail. Others were called upon to go through severe tests and trials. The Lord knows exactly what each of us needs so that He can stamp His own image upon us. His way is perfect. It is far better to have Him put us through the refining fires than to come up short when we see Him face to face. He knows what each Christian needs to face and will not put more on us than we can bear.

I know that in my whirlwind of fear, the Lord came to me with His Word and made His peace triumph in my heart and life. "Thou hast also given me the shield of thy salvation: and thy right hand hath holden me up, and thy gentleness hath made me great. Thou hast enlarged my steps under me, that my feet did not slip." (Psalm 18:35,36) Again, it is grace! We cannot claim anything in our salvation—it was the supernatural power of Jesus who loved us and gave Himself for us.

As the day of my surgery drew nearer, I clearly knew that I must put my soul and body into the hands of a faithful Creator. (We should be doing this every day, anyway.) He was and is the only One who can take care of me. My family did everything in their power to assure me of their prayers, love, and support and this meant so very much to me. I've never seen anyone support a wife and mother as my family did. Family and friends agonized in prayer for me, and cards, e-mail messages, and phone calls assured me of continuing intercession.

What a wonderful Lord we have! He brought me through surgery safely, the tumor was benign, and after only four days in the hospital, I was able to go home. I'm on medication for six months, and even though I had to take sleeping pills for a time, my sleeping patterns are becoming more normal. I have learned not to question or judge those who have to take medication. The Lord is merciful and He doesn't condemn us just because our bodies are going through traumatic experiences. He *was* with me and *is* with me through all my struggles, and this is a lesson I needed to learn.

It is interesting to me that the Lord gives us the faith and grace we need at the particular time we need it. In Hebrews chapter 11 we read of several patriarchs of faith: Abel, Enoch, Noah, Abraham and Sarah, Isaac and Jacob, Joseph, Moses and his parents, Joshua, Rahab, and a number of others who received faith *when they needed it.* Notice that Jacob and

Joseph received dying faith at the time they needed it—an example that the Lord will provide exactly what we need at the proper time.

It is better to *trust in the Lord* than to turn from Him when trials come. When we cast ourselves on the mercy of God, we are in the safest place, because He will not fail us. Now that I've been through the operation and the Lord has brought me through with victory over doubt and fear in this matter, I need His guidance and help more than ever.

I'm glad the Lord watches out for His own; He doesn't just leave us to chance. Most of my Christian life I had let the enemy discourage me when trials came along. I felt that the Lord was disappointed in me and I had to seek Him to get back in a right relationship with Him. I never doubted God's Word; my problem was doubting that I had done all I was supposed to do for God's approval. He taught me that there is *nothing* I can do except accept Him and what He did at Calvary.

Let me say that I realize not everyone has the same medical results I did; some have cancer and are devastated. The point of my testimony is not that everyone's victory will be the same as mine but that *all can trust God, no matter what happens*. The Lord knows the reasons for our trials and He also knows how to give the victory that will bring Him glory and honor.

When the victory is God's, we cannot claim any glory for ourselves. That's really the way it should be, anyway. I'm thankful the Lord loves us enough to keep working in our lives to cause us to produce the fruit He wants. It takes a longsuffering and merciful Savior to teach us His way. In every valley experience and every victory the Lord gives, may we give Him the glory!

> "But God forbid that I should glory, save in the cross of our Lord Jesus Christ, by whom the world is crucified unto me, and I unto the world." (Galatians 6:14)

## What Cancer Cannot Do!

Cancer took the life of my father when he was only 48 years old but back in the 50's cancer wasn't talked about—it was all hush-hush. I was 21, married and carrying my first child, and up until then my life had been idyllic. The cancer struck quickly and my father's death left me bitter. I had had a wonderful relationship with my grandfather and my child would be deprived of the love of a grandpa. I definitely was not happy about it!

I had received Christ as my personal Savior when I was a teenager, but Dad's death puzzled me and made me question God. I felt He was cruel and uncaring, common emotions in the face of loss, I suppose. However, my relationship with my heavenly Father was damaged.

Within a couple of years, my mother remarried and six years later my stepfather was found to have cancer. He lived for another two years and his death threw me into even more of a state of confusion about God. I just couldn't understand how a loving God could allow this horrible disease to strike both my fathers.

During the next twenty years, several close friends in our church died of cancer. At that time chemotherapy and radiation were not widely used to curb the effects of this disease. I felt that I had a special empathy for people with cancer because of how close it had hit my family.

In 1994 my own husband, Irving, faced cancer. By now he was retired and we had plans for our future, which included moving to a warmer climate. Just two weeks before our planned move, Irving got violently ill and medical examination revealed a bowel obstruction. Surgery and a colostomy followed and our personal plans were put on hold.

During this ordeal, we enjoyed so many blessings from the Lord that it's hard to enumerate them all. Friends provided us a peaceful country home where Irving could recuperate and someone else offered to pay our medical bills. We didn't have insurance because after Irving retired it just seemed too expensive. We had a track record of good health and soon we would be eligible for Medicare insurance—and we got stuck in the middle, not at all prepared for the enormous medical costs.

We were able to make the move to the warmer climate and within a few months, Irving had his colostomy reversed. At that time they found that the cancer had spread to his lymph nodes, so chemotherapy was necessary. Once again loving friends supported us, and some rocky family relationships were healed.

The new medical bills loomed heavy over us and we cashed in Irving's IRA to pay part of the hospital bill. We decided we could slowly and painfully pay down the debt, no matter how long it took, and help came from many sources. We found that we had sown into so many lives that God was now using these same people to bless us. It was a humbling experience, as we learned that it is harder to receive than to give! Irving has been completely healed and cancer-free for eight years. Praise God.

A couple of years ago we felt led to move back to the north to be close to our daughter and our only grandchildren. Truly God was in our decision, because that fall our daughter had to undergo a mastectomy and aggressive treatment. The chemotherapy and radiation completely consumed her life for nine months, while we remained confident that she would be completely healed. We were comforted by the Word of God and personal words of encouragement from people. Friends surrounded her with loving comfort, and we stood alongside the family through this tough time. One again God proved to be so faithful—and our daughter is now cancer-free.

In the spring of 2000, a sonogram and CT scan revealed a tumor on my left kidney, and a number of complications developed. On Good Friday I remembered how our Lord had suffered for my sake, so I knew that I could endure all that was happening in my body. I knew His great love would sustain me and I was feeling quite peaceful and confident. But my trials weren't over yet.

Shingles attacked my left lower back and leg and what misery that brought. One morning I woke up with a slogan running through my mind, planted there by God: No Fear— Just Cheer! Other words and prayers sustained me through the weeks prior to the surgery on my kidney. My children flew in, and I was showered with gifts, cards, and phone calls. I was especially blessed by the visits of my pastor and his wife.

A wonderful, skilled surgeon carved a golf ball-sized tumor out of my left kidney. The night before surgery, the Lord came to me with a bowl of heavenly manna and told me, "Take and eat." I believed it was a sign that I would be healed and truly I did have a remarkable recovery—especially for a woman over 70! It was the first surgery I had ever had, and the last, I hope.

Today Irving and I, along with our daughter, are part of a Cancer Support Group. We share about the healing power of Jesus and the joy of the Lord to the people who attend the meetings. We use our experiences to give the hope of Christ to others who are walking down similar paths. Scripture, slogans, poems, and books of encouragement are shared. Cancer cannot kill the spirit of man! We can overcome by the blood of the Lamb and the word of our testimony. We are not victims—but survivors! Praise the Lord.

Here is one of several inspirational pieces that have guided us through our experiences with cancer.

WHAT CANCER CANNOT DO
Cancer is so limited!
It cannot cripple love!
It cannot shatter hope,
It cannot corrode faith,
It cannot destroy peace,
It cannot kill friendship,
It cannot suppress memories,
It cannot silence courage,
It cannot invade the soul,
It cannot steal eternal life,
It cannot conquer the spirit!

Our family's journey through cancer has been difficult, but since the baptism in the Spirit, we have received added power and strength to walk through any trial in life. We have felt God's healing power and know that He is able to do all things!

## I Chose Life

I have a long history with cancer, both as a caregiver and a survivor. My father's life was taken by cancer when he was only 47 years old, but before he died he accepted Jesus into his heart. His final days were full of singing, praying, and reading the Word, and his victory in the face of death was a marvelous gift to his family.

Only one week after my father died, my husband, Andrew, had to have a tumor removed from his neck. When tests showed a malignancy, I was thrown into a state of panic. We had three young children and such uncertainty about my husband's future totally unnerved me.

I went outside on one of those early spring days and noticed life springing out of the huge, old maple tree in our yard. I picked one of the new leaves, held it in my hand and asked, "Lord, will Andrew and I see another spring together?" My heart was breaking and searching for answers.

I went back into the house to answer the phone; it was one of my friends from Bible study. I shared my concerns with her and she responded, "Christina, commit your life to the Lord." Andrew and I *did* commit our lives to the Lord and today, thirty-two years later, my husband still loves to tell his story.

Next, just four years after Andrew's illness, his grandmother died of lung cancer, and then his dear old grandfather came to live with us—and he also faced cancer. Caring for him was difficult, but we had the great joy of sharing Jesus with him and he accepted Christ into his life. Six months later he died.

Unbelievably, our family still was not finished with cancer. Just a short time after Grandpa died, my mother brought awful news. One morning when I answered the doorbell, there stood my sister and my mother, her face filled with pain.

"Mother, what is it?" I asked.

"I've just been to the doctor," she replied. "I have cancer and I'm going to die."

I took her by the hand and led her to the back of our home. "Mother, you could leave here in your car and be struck by another car and die," I told her. "Your life could be over just that quickly. Are you ready to go home to be with the Lord? Do you have the assurance of your salvation in Jesus Christ?"

Oh, the joy that filled our hearts as Mother prayed with me to receive Christ into her heart. Yes, she did fight cancer for two years and went through some unpleasant treatments. But she trusted in the Lord daily and lived a totally surrendered life before she experienced the ultimate healing: a glorified, painless, supernatural body.

In 1993 my dear friend, Kathryn, was diagnosed with breast cancer and I thought my heart would break. I watched her faith and trust grow as she leaned on the Lord in her battle, and today she remains cancer-free.

In the summer of 1998, I also was diagnosed with breast cancer. A tumor was growing on my chest wall, very similar to the condition my mother had. On hearing this news, I lost my will to fight—I just wanted to go home to be with the Lord. I felt like cancer had delivered too many blows to our family.

One of the struggles I had with my own cancer was the fear of the treatment; I felt that it would be worse than the disease itself. I started trying to figure out a timeline. If I could just live to see the birth of our youngest daughter's first child, due in a couple of months, that would be good enough. As is often the case, God had another plan!

After service one Sunday, I stood with my husband outside the church talking to a dear friend. As we chatted, God gave me a vision of our daughter, Ashley, walking by me carrying a child wrapped in a white blanket. Her first child was walking alongside her, tugging at her hemline, and it hit me! "I don't want to miss the blessing of seeing our grandchildren reared in a Christian home." Right then and there *I chose life* and decided to fight for it!

> "I have set before you life and death, blessing and cursing: therefore choose life, that thou and thy seed may live." (Deuteronomy 30:19)

As the months passed, Ashley had her second child and God's vision was fulfilled. His grace brings great joy in times of trial and testing.

When my daughter, Morgan, learned I had cancer, she asked, "Mother, if there was one thing you would like to do, what would it be?"

My response was, "My dream-come-true would be to visit Times Square Church in New York City."

Well, of course, my family saw to it that I visited the church and I'll never forget that first visit. Before Pastor Wilkerson preached, the congregation read a Scripture that the Lord had impressed on me 27 years earlier: "...the desert shall rejoice, and blossom as a rose." (Isaiah 35:1) My spirit soared with JOY and I knew the desert and the dry ground would bring forth fruit.

I returned with my family to Times Square Church the day before I was to begin a series of 33 radiation treatments. The church had a healing service, and people wanting prayer were urged to come to the front. I went forward, Bible in hand, and told the pastor I had cancer. I also told him I was standing on the Word: "I shall not die, but live, and declare the works of the Lord." (Psalm 118:17) He prayed with me and I returned to my seat.

In His mercy and love, God ministered to me through Exodus 15:26: "I am the Lord that healeth thee, I will heal thee." God's Word brought life and healing to my soul, and through the fellowship of believers, I experienced God's healing power.

I walked through the valley of the shadow of death, but I did not fear evil. The words of Psalm 23 were life to me:

"The Lord is my shepherd; I shall not want. He maketh me to lie down in green pastures; He leadeth me beside the still waters, He restoreth my soul."

"When thou passest through the waters, I will be with thee; and through the rivers, they shall not overflow thee: when thou walketh through the fire, thou shalt not be burned; neither shall the flame kindle upon thee." (Isaiah 43:2)

When I began radiation, God encouraged me with this Scripture out of Isaiah. I went through three months of painful, aggressive therapy; months of testing to see if there was any metastasis; three surgical procedures within a five-month period that caused me to drop down to 92 pounds; the partial removal of six ribs; nine months of fighting infection; three months of physical therapy; and three months of casting and fitting for a prosthesis. And I'm still here to tell my story!

God brought me through all of this and gave me a peace that truly passes all understanding. I was often encouraged by the life of Job. God had a plan for his life and it was better than anything Job could have visualized during the time he was facing adversity. The second half of Job's life was greater than the first.

Jesus Christ gave me power to endure great pain and although the healing process was slow, I am happy I chose life and fought for it. I have entered into His JOY in suffering.

"The Spirit Himself bears witness with our spirit that we are children of God, and if children, then heirs— heirs of God and joint-heirs with Christ; if so be that we suffer with Him, that we may be also glorified together. For I reckon that the sufferings of this present time are not worthy to be compared with the glory which shall be revealed in us." (Romans 8:16-18)

Throughout my ordeal, God blessed me with compassionate surgeons and competent medical personnel, a dear family who lovingly cared for me, and wonderful, praying friends. I experienced a depth of love I did not know existed, and I found that God's grace is sufficient to meet all our needs. His power is made perfect in our time of weakness.

I have experienced the healing touch of Jesus Christ, the Great Physician, and recent tests confirm that I am cancer-free.

## The Doctor Laughed So Hard He Almost Fell Out of His Chair

Many years ago our pastor noticed a lump on his waist near his belt buckle and made a mental note to get it checked; he thought it was a hernia. Because he drove a school bus to augment his salary, he decided to wait until spring break to have the hernia checked so he wouldn't have to miss any work.

Pastor Stillwell loved driving that school bus and the students loved him. He considered the bus a mission field, and he did all he could to minister to the precious, lost teenagers and children.

When Pastor finally went to the doctor to have the hernia surgically removed, he wasn't prepared for the report he heard. The head surgeon said, "We don't really know how to tell you this, but here goes! You are nothing but cancer from your neck all the way down to your navel. You have at least 500 pencil eraser-sized tumors in your lungs and the thing you thought was a hernia actually is a tumor the size of an orange."

What followed was a blur of tests and surgeries. A tumor was discovered on his aorta and another tumor had blocked off one of his kidneys, leaving him with only one functioning kidney. After the surgeons had removed as many of the tumors as they could, they informed Pastor Stillwell, "We are going to give you radiation therapy to try to buy you some time."

"What kind of time are you talking about?" Pastor asked.

"Well, with the radiation, we can give you about six months to live; without it, we won't give you six weeks."

Pastor Stillwell went ahead with the first treatment, but it made him so sick he prayed to die right there in the treatment center. That night, after the effects of the treatment wore off, he was praying and the Lord spoke to him. "If you will do what I tell you, you won't be sick anymore."

"Yes, Lord, You know I'll do anything not to be so sick. What is it?"

"You know I have chosen the foolish things of the world to confound the wise and this may sound foolish. Tomorrow

I want you to tell the doctor that I told you to take a teaspoon-ful of Pepto-Bismol before each radiation treatment and you won't get sick."

Well, a little argument ensued because, frankly, Pastor Stillwell wasn't so sure he wanted to tell the doctors what the Lord had told him. "Lord, couldn't I just take the Pepto-Bismol, then tell the doctors about it later?" But God wouldn't hear any of that!

When Pastor got to the doctor's office, he said, "Doctor, God spoke something to me last night."

"Oh, He did, did He? And what was that?"

"He told me to tell you that if I take a teaspoonful of Pepto-Bismol before each radiation treatment, I won't get sick again."

The doctor laughed so hard he almost fell out of his chair! "Pastor Stillwell, this is cobalt radiation therapy, not a stom-achache!"

"Well, that's what God said, and He told me to tell you."

"Do whatever you think you have to do—and let's get started."

The victorious end of this testimony is that Pastor Stillwell didn't get sick anymore. He didn't lose any hair and his white blood cell count did exactly the opposite of the "usual" dur-ing radiation. Toward the end of the treatment, x-rays were taken and the technicians rushed out to get him, almost laugh-ing in their excitement. "Pastor, Pastor, look at this!"

He looked but since he wasn't trained to read x-rays, he didn't really know what he was looking at. "What is it?" he asked. The technicians got the doctor to come look at the x-ray and he expressed amazement.

"Don't you see it? Don't you see it? There's not any scar tissue! You've got something in your blood that cures cancer and we're going to find out what it is!"

Needless to say, Pastor Stillwell knew what had happened

and he quickly told the staff, "I've got the same blood as all of you have. Jesus has healed me by *His* blood!"

Still, the doctor wasn't convinced and he had blood drawn from Pastor Stillwell. Then he sent samples of the blood to several prestigious research hospitals around the nation to have it analyzed. He must have thought he had discovered some miracle cure—still not recognizing the *real* Miracle Cure.

The reports on the blood samples came back with the same report: normal blood. And that in itself was a miracle.

God brought our pastor through and we have seen first-hand an example of obedience in doing what God tells you to do!

## "We Doctors Are Just His Instruments"

My Catholic training told me that I wasn't capable of interpreting the Word of God—the priest would do that for me. At mass I would hear short, selected readings of the Bible, but that was all I knew of it. However, I read some writings of a Unity minister, and she introduced me to the idea of *affirmative prayer*. I was not walking with the Lord, but without knowing it, I was learning something valuable that would help me during one of my darkest hours.

In 1988, when my son was sixteen, he was brutally beaten by some boys after a football game. They left him lying on the road about two blocks from our home and when he was found, he was barely breathing. When he got to the hospital, he was immediately placed on a ventilator for life support.

My neighbor called me at work to tell me that Tony was in serious condition at the local hospital. I became so weak I could hardly walk and I was too shaken to drive. A friend drove me the long twenty minutes to the hospital—a trip that seemed to take hours. I began repeating over and over, "Jesus

Christ is healing Tony now." I pictured Jesus standing at my son's bed and both of them were surrounded by light. Remember, I did not know Jesus but I had been learning some basic principles of trusting Him and I was blessed with great faith. I asked my friend if he would join me in affirmative prayer and he said he didn't believe, but he would call on the name of Jesus with me anyway.

At that point I had no idea what had happened to Tony. I feared he had been shot or stabbed. I was a nurse and I knew that when they bypassed our little neighborhood hospital where I worked and headed for the trauma center, it was very serious.

When I arrived at the hospital, my ex-husband and the trauma surgeon told me Tony might die. I remember the disbelief I felt when the doctor told me he wasn't breathing on his own. He had suffered severe head trauma and the next twenty-four hours would be crucial. After calling my family, I called some of the nurses where I worked and asked them to pray for Tony. I knew that some of them were God-fearing people and I needed their help.

I sat in the waiting room all night repeating like a mantra, "Jesus Christ is healing Tony now." My twenty-four-year-old daughter was hysterical when she arrived at the hospital so I got her in on the action. "Vickie, repeat these words with me," I said and she calmed down. The words seemed to have a soothing, reassuring effect on her. Jesus was with us even though we weren't really "doing it right." But we were doing the best we could.

Two nurses came to visit from my place of employment and one of them gave me her "Nurse Bible"—a Gideon New Testament distributed to hospital staff. As I said, I never read the Bible but that little Book became like life support to me. I gained the strength I needed to hear the doctor's constant grim reports. I read about Jesus healing so many sick ones and I saw that He healed the ones that had *faith*. The more I read the Word, the stronger my faith became.

When Tony was twelve, he visited a Pentecostal church with friends and attended quite regularly. He began to read the Bible and eventually gave his heart to Jesus. I admit he asked me over and over again to go to church with him, but I always refused by saying, "Son, we're Catholic! If I attend a church, it's going to be Catholic." Tony continued to read the Word and grow in the Lord. He told me that my astrology books and fortune-telling expeditions were of the devil, but I never believed him. Then, as my son lay close to death, I began seeing that same truth in the Bible.

I would go into the trauma unit three times a day to see my precious son. I prayed for him there but when the pain became unbearable, I'd clutch my Bible close and rush to the chapel. There I would cry out to the Lord and He always heard me—I knew He heard me. Although I was not yet walking with the Lord, He was walking with me!

One of my neighbors who knew the Bible very well made regular visits to the hospital. She would point out God's promises to me and encourage me to seek Him. My little New Testament soon had so many scraps of paper (bookmarks) in it that I could instantly find the inspirational Scriptures when I desperately needed them. God had His hand on me!

One night a woman I had not seen in fifteen years called me from out of state. She said God had given her a message for me while she was at a prayer meeting, then she directed me to a verse in the Bible. Whenever I was down, God picked me up! On another occasion, Tony's fever was edging up close to 105 degrees and I was sitting by his bed at 3 o'clock in the morning, crying. A doctor walked by and stopped. "Sister, why are you crying and holding the Bible? Don't you know that God is the Alpha and Omega? He can do anything! We doctors are just His instruments. Don't listen to our words, listen to His Word!" I knew once again that Jesus was with me.

Tony was a quarterback on his high school football team and the boys on the team were very close. His friends came down at night after practice to visit him and they would end up encouraging me. We would go to the chapel, hold hands, and pray. I would tell them about God's Word and I also told them that I knew He would raise Tony up if we believed. One of the young men, Matt, told me that he had trained with my son all summer and he knew how strong he was. He also mentioned Tony's strong faith in Jesus. "Don't ever give up on Jesus and Tony." I'll never forget those words, and I knew that Jesus heard us as we prayed on those dark nights.

We saw few changes in Tony's condition and the doctors were not very hopeful, but deep in my heart I knew he would awaken. Sure enough, thirteen days after "the incident," Tony suddenly woke up and said, "I'm hungry!" He had lost forty pounds, he couldn't walk, and he could barely see, but he was awake! I walked over to him and said, "Tony, Jesus Christ healed you," and he gave me the "thumbs up" sign. He fully understood.

Tony remained in the hospital for a little over three months, then spent another three months in rehabilitation therapy. Today, my son has no cognitive, physical, or neurological deficits. Praise God! Thank You, Jesus!

When Tony was in rehab, he was allowed to come home for weekends. The first weekend at home, he asked me to go to church with him—I would have gone *anywhere* with him! Although he could barely walk, we slowly made it to church, and I have been going back to that church ever since.

Patiently the Holy Spirit instructed me and very soon I took that long walk up the aisle and accepted Jesus into my heart. I truly am a new creation and I owe it all to the Word of God. That little Nurse Bible was the beginning because it gave me hope when there was no hope. "Affirmative prayer" could only go so far; the power was in the Word of God! His

Word strengthened me and sustained me through the darkest nights of my entire life. Truly, God is close to us when our hearts are breaking.

## Dying from the Dye

Last year Nate began to have symptoms that seemed to indicate a gall bladder attack. He landed in the hospital for a battery of tests that showed absolutely nothing. Our local doctor had several ideas of what was wrong, but he sent him to a specialist who recommended a test involving a dye. Things went well and Nate was sent home with a list of "side effects" to watch for. We were told that about one in every hundred persons has a "reaction" to the dye used in the test— and thus began our saga of Nate's "dye experience."

The morning following the test, Nate experienced nausea during breakfast, a usual side effect of the dye. He called the doctor, who told him he might be experiencing the first symptoms of pancreatitis. The doctor put the emergency room on alert for Nate's arrival and we got ready as quickly as we could. By the time I got dressed, Nate was in such pain that he could hardly stand, so we opted to go to our smaller emergency room, which was closer to where we lived. We had all the essential information to give to the ER doctors so that Nate could receive treatment, but the local staff made him suffer needlessly for three hours while they performed their own tests—and came up with the same results. This kind of thing causes so much stress! Nate begged for something to relieve his pain, but was denied until the doctors got their results. Anyway, Nate finally got limited relief from morphine and was admitted to the hospital.

For days Nate was seriously ill and received regular injections of morphine to try to control his pain. He became so jaundiced that the whites of his eyes were golden yellow. After eight days he was released from the hospital and he eventually returned to work, but he didn't fully recover. He lost so much weight that people thought he had cancer but just wouldn't tell them the truth.

About three months later, Nate started to run a high fever, and blood work determined that he had a urinary tract infection. Antibiotics made him feel better, but I knew something wasn't right. The doctor told me Nate was a very sick man and it might take as long as a year for him to fully recover. I think the doctor was trying to tell me to stop bugging him and be more patient with Nate's slow progress. However, as soon as he went off his antibiotics, the fever returned, so he was prescribed another round of antibiotics.

His regular check-up time arrived during this round of antibiotics, and this is when we found out that something definitely was not right. The doctor said he wanted Nate to see a specialist again and he even made us wait in his office until the appointment was made. We thought we were just going in for drainage tubes, a minor outpatient procedure that would help drain infection from Nate's body.

The procedure was scheduled for Thursday and I met Nate for lunch that Wednesday. I watched from the restaurant as he walked up the stairs. My husband was a man I no longer recognized! He had lost so much weight his shoulder blades were prominent under his shirt, and he was hunched over like a very old man. His voice was weak and he was ashen-faced. I realized I hadn't seen my "real" husband for many weeks. He left the restaurant quickly (no energy) and I returned to work very concerned. As soon as I got back to my office, Nate was on the phone telling me we had to go to the hospital that very evening—we couldn't wait until the next day. I was definitely worried.

We went to the hospital and after seeing several doctors, we finally got some action. They were going to do surgery at one o'clock in the morning, but they wouldn't tell us exactly what was wrong with Nate. Three different times doctors came in and told us that Nate didn't look as sick as he was (and I thought he looked pretty sick). One doctor, whom I dubbed "Dr. Grim" because she was so pessimistic, talked to us like she wanted to be sure we had no hope that Nate would make it through surgery alive, much less ever leave the hospital.

It was not my practice to put God to the test, because it seemed like such a brazen thing to do, but I desperately needed something tangible to hang on to. Yes, I had faith, but at that moment I felt like I needed a sign that Nate was going to make it through all this. That's when the miracles started happening.

Miracle Number One: Nate's doctor came in and said that as ill as he was, he should already be dead. I accepted this as God's way of assuring me that no matter how bad things looked, I needed to trust Him to take care of Nate. He was going to get through this! God had given Nate a wonderful body and he was going to survive in spite of the severity of his illness. After all, if he "should already be dead," then he was already defying medical odds.

Dr. Grim then delivered her message of doom regarding the pending surgery. She told us that Nate could possibly bleed to death on the operating table because the vessels to the spleen had been blocked by the infection, causing blood to build up, much like an aneurysm. Then she told us he could have a stroke or heart attack during surgery. Or the infection could cause kidney failure, resulting in his death. Or his pancreas could be so damaged by the infection that it would be useless, resulting in death. So many ways for Nate to die! She told us that the mortality rate in this surgery was extremely high—in fact, she told us this three times. There was no good news coming from this doctor!

Miracle Number Two: Nate survived the surgery! But doom and gloom followed. His pancreas had been so damaged by the infection that they had to remove part of it. His spleen had to be removed, and he had to have a colostomy because they found a hole in his colon. Also, he had to receive ten units of blood and this is always scary. But the good news was that if he survived the night (and even though he still would be a very ill man), they would put him on a respirator for at least two weeks and "keep him going."

Miracle Number Three: After his surgery, Nate was put on a respirator, but they noted that over half his breaths were made on his own. So *the very next day*, they took him off the respirator!

Miracle Number Four: He had to be taken to the Intensive Care Unit, of course, but the miracle is that he survived there. The nurse told me that when they wheeled him in, she was told that he wouldn't make it through the night.

Miracle Number Five: He stayed in ICU only three days because, as the nurse put it, "There was no physical reason he should be here."

Miracle Number Six: He was home in ten days—not the many weeks that had been predicted.

Miracle Number Seven: We finally got Dr. Grim to halfway admit that Nate's recovery actually was a miracle of God.

All of Nate's misery was the result of a liquid dye that was used in a fairly routine test. This kind of experience leaves you very wary of some medical procedures.

Nate is recovering and we feel so blessed by God. His life was spared due to the prayers of many saints of God and we give Him all the glory. This experience has made a great impact on our lives.

A very dear friend who stood by us throughout this ordeal said, "We not only believe in miracles, we expect them!" And we depend on them, too!

# PART TWO

# ABANDONMENT

## Abandoned — But Not Forsaken!

After serving the Lord and pastoring several churches for over thirty-five years, my husband left me for a young married woman in our church. In an instant, two families were completely traumatized and the precious people who attended the church were shocked and saddened by the moral failure of the pastor they loved and trusted.

I was numb with grief and devastation. About all I could do was cry out to God, "Why, Lord? Why? I've served You with all my heart since I was a girl, and I've been true to You all these years. I have tried to show Your love and kindness to everyone and I've never compromised Your Word. I have even taught Your Word faithfully for years. Why, Lord, have You allowed this to happen to me?"

At nearly sixty years of age, I was completely stripped of everything. I had lost my husband and my source of income, and I had a medical condition that incapacitated me. I became emaciated and was slowly dying. Of course, I couldn't work, and to top it off, I was three years away from being able to draw Social Security payments. I was completely over-whelmed—what was I going to do?

When my husband resigned his pastorate, I lost my church family as well as my ministerial family. I was haunted by the realization that the dear church people who had always been so good to us could have been a source of comfort and sup-port, but they were gone. The ministerial family that had pro-vided wonderful fellowship, locally as well as on the district and national level, was gone, as well. Simply put, I had lost my identity as a pastor's wife. Gone! I was out! I felt aban-doned by everyone, and yes, even by God. I felt like a big glob of clay at the feet of Jesus—stripped of everything and terribly broken.

After months of weeping, heart-searching, and asking God over and over why He had allowed this to happen to me, I felt His presence draw me near. It happened at the end of my regular prayer time as I sat quietly on the floor by the couch, which I often did, giving God an opportunity to speak to my heart. One last "why?" escaped my lips—and then I sensed the *awesome presence of God.*

I did not see Jesus with my physical eyes, but I knew He was there. I felt so comforted and peaceful, and enveloped in pure love. I began to weep softly, then I whispered, "Lord, I didn't know the human heart could hurt so badly. Will You please tell me why You allowed such hurt and pain in my life?" In my inner spirit I heard the Lord say to me, "Child, I'm beginning to answer the prayer you prayed in the prayer room when you were a student at Bible college years ago."

I was shocked when I heard that! How well I remembered that day when, as a 20-year-old girl, I was alone in the prayer room seeking God. A deep yearning, which I believe was birthed by the Holy Spirit, caused me to sincerely pray, "Lord, I really want to know Your heart." Then I prayed Paul's prayer, "That I may know him, and the power of his resurrection, and the fellowship of his sufferings, being made conformable unto his death." (Philippians 3:10)

At that time, many years ago, I had absolutely no comprehension of what the deep, costly significance of that verse was. I just knew it came from a sincere heart that wanted to know the heart of God. Now, forty years later, surrounded by the breathtaking presence of God, I received a divine illumination of why He had allowed me to experience such depths of sorrow and pain. He was answering my prayer and helping me learn something about His heart.

It became very clear to me that my deep grief and pain of betrayal and rejection by someone I loved and trusted brought me into the "fellowship of His sufferings." I cried out to Him, "Lord, I didn't realize how much pain Your broken heart experienced when You were rejected by those You loved. Lord, forgive me for the times I've caused You pain."

I realized that being stripped of everything, and being shamed and embarrassed like my precious Lord, was what it meant to be made "conformable unto His death." My will had to be fully surrendered to His divine will—only then could He be LORD! Through my tears I asked the Lord to allow my heart to be grieved with those things that grieve His heart. I don't ever want to hurt the heart of God again, for I have learned in a small measure how much God grieves when we ignore Him or treat Him lightly.

The Lord communicated to me that morning, "You will now begin to see through My eyes and see what I see, not what others might see. You will begin to hear through My ears what I hear. Not the coarse language or the raucous laughter but, rather, the cry coming from the heart of a soul that is lost or hurting."

One of the most sobering things the Lord said to me, although He said it with much love and tenderness, was, "You've been so busy working FOR Me that you haven't always worked WITH Me. I want you to work WITH Me in the yoke of My will. Doing what others ask you to do or expect you to do is not necessarily what I want you to do." I asked His forgiveness for that.

I wonder how many pastors and church leaders are guilty of this. On the other hand, how many lay people place demands upon pastors and leaders to do things that God has not asked them to do? All of us need to be yoked together with Christ to do what *He,* not *man,* orders.

Several months after that experience with the Lord, I was rushed to the hospital near death. I felt my life slipping away due to the chronic intestinal disease I had suffered from for years, but the doctors were able to stabilize me. A pastor and his wife came to see me in the hospital; they were visiting in the area and had heard that I was seriously ill. When they walked into my room, the pastor said, "Dear Sister, I have a word from God for you! You're not through; your ministry is not through; and God is going to give you a healthy body with which to enjoy it."

The following day another dear saint gave me practically the same message. Then the next day, early in the morning when I was just beginning to awaken, I heard the voice of the Holy Spirit speak the following words: "Rise up, my love, my fair one, and come away. For lo, the winter is past, the rain is over and gone; the flowers appear on the earth; and the time of the singing of birds is come…(Song of Solomon 2:10-12) It's a new day for you!"

Three days and three messages from God to my soul! Paul tells us, "In the mouth of two or three witnesses shall every word be established." (II Corinthians 13:1) Those messages given to me in the hospital have come to pass. For eleven years now, my yearly physicals have shown no sign of the intestinal disease in my body. Not only that but, like David, I can say, "He hath filled my mouth with laughter and my tongue with singing." (Psalm 126:2) My ministry in the body of Christ has become more fruitful and the joy of the Lord is my strength. God has kept His Word to this little grandma. May He ever be praised!

## I Felt Like a Train Hit Me —<br>Where Was God?

The Bible study group my husband and I started grew into a thriving church, which we pastored for nine years. Our only child, a son, graduated from a major Christian university and helped us in the church for a couple of years. We were all pleased when he announced his engagement to a lovely Christian girl in May, setting the wedding for the next May.

Three months after that announcement, my husband told me he no longer loved me and was leaving right after our son's wedding, which was still nine months away. Our son lived with us and in order not to mar his happy plans, we kept this secret between the two of us—we did, however, share it with two trusted board members in the church.

Need I say that I was in shock? My heart was crushed and I felt like a train hit me and then, before I could get off the tracks, another train going the other direction hit me. My son's wedding day was truly the most difficult day of my life, as I knew that when I returned home, I would lose everything. Sadly, there was no one I could talk to about it, but God sustained me, giving me peace, and even joy, at a time when my heart was truly broken in pieces.

My husband kept his "promise" and after our son was married, he pulled out of our driveway with all his belongings in his car. It seemed like he had a complete breakdown at the age of 49, suffered what is commonly referred to as a "midlife crisis," and walked out on his life. He moved to another state, six hours from where we lived, and went to work for an insurance company.

Four months later, two of my husband's best friends divorced each other; she had been a counselor on staff at our church and her husband had been a board member. She felt that the Lord "led" her to move to the town where my husband was working, so he moved her out there and set her up in an apartment right next to his.

During this time I was struggling to make sense of everything. I had lost my identity and had a hard time functioning in the "real world." My husband had always taken care of all the details of life in our home, so I had some major adjusting to do.

A few years later, my husband divorced me and, after 32 years of marriage, I felt *really alone.* Within the year, my now ex-husband married the lady who had moved next door to him.

I was born again and Spirit-filled, but I came to realize that *I really didn't know Jesus!* In my search for a deeper knowledge of Him, I went through fire and crushing. Through it all, He taught me to persevere, endure, tenaciously walk in faith, and trust Him. I know that He has everything under control and has only my best interest at heart. A wonderful and miraculous transformation has taken place in my life and I am a brand-new person. I thank God for loving me so much that He allowed me to walk through the fire so I could know Him intimately and have this tremendous loving relationship with Him. I was blind and now I see clearly!

I asked the Lord to take out all the garbage, trash, junk, and debris in me. I prayed for Him to mold me and shape me into the image of Jesus. I continue to ask Him to make me a godly woman, a woman of honesty and integrity, radically obedient and sold out to Him. I want an impeccable reputation, not compromising the Word, not giving the appearance of evil or causing anyone to stumble. I desire to be a woman who walks in the image of Jesus Christ, a witness for Him and Him only.

The Lord placed in me the desire to be a speaker and I thought I would be speaking on overcoming depression, then separation, then "the other woman," then divorce, and then remarriage. I now know that people will be hearing how to come into a deeper relationship with the Lord Jesus Christ, learning to focus on Him and allowing Him to have every-thing in our lives. Everything is possible with God! He can and will do miraculous changes in our lives when we allow Him to literally take over. This happens when we learn to take our hands off so He can do whatever is necessary to transform us into the image of His Son, Jesus.

Mine has been an incredible journey. It is one that I cer-tainly would not want to repeat, but I am so thankful God allowed it because of the person I have become in Him. I truly know who I am in Christ. I live in joy, rest, contentment, peace, and victory—and I would not trade it for anything!

## The Mailbox Contained $2,000 in Cash!

When my boys were only two and five years old, my hus-band left me for his secretary. I had a little formal education, but no degree, and I struggled to support the boys. To make matters worse, I fell into severe depression and turned to al-cohol. The divorce took four long years and then there was a custody battle, which, by the grace of God, I won. However, by that time my drinking problem was serious and I was not able to function as a normal human being.

My wonderful and faithful mother and father mobilized a prayer chain that stretched across the entire nation, and in His mercy, God saved my life. My parents extended them-selves far beyond anything I deserved, but their love and sup-port helped me salvage my life and my family. I was able to get out-of-state custody of the boys and we moved in with my parents. I had a demon-possessed boyfriend, but after I got away from him, I turned my life completely over to the Lord. At that point my sons were eight and ten.

After two years with my folks, I felt strong enough to break away on my own again. I put my trust in the Lord, and the boys and I moved to a town about three hours from my parents. We continued to go through some tough times, but I did my best to be a good provider—and I prayed a lot. There were times we were out of food and we would find groceries on our front step! At times someone else paid the rent. The most spectacular instance of His provision happened the day I saw a rainbow across the entire sky. I had always felt that rainbows signify promise, and when I checked the mailbox that day, there was $2,000 in cash! To this day we don't know who sent it—but we know God provided it!

I was devoted to my children and I put a lot of effort into training them. I was strict with them and always made sure I was home when they got home. I also made sure I knew where they were at all times. God blessed my efforts and the boys grew up to be very popular in high school. They both excelled in sports and maintained good testimonies for the Lord.

Both my sons received scholarships to college and they worked hard. My older son graduated and is now married to a wonderful Christian woman. My younger son will receive his degree in May—and he's waiting for a Christian woman. I thank God for them both.

I could not have made it without completely giving my sons up to the Lord. He guarded and protected us as we struggled through life. It truly is a miracle that we made it and I owe a great debt of gratitude to the many people who prayed for us, especially my parents. I know without a doubt that prayer made the difference! I want to always remember what He has done for me and will continue to do.

# PART THREE

# CHILDREN

## Death at Columbine!

My sister, Dee, and I were very close. She and her husband had led me to the Lord and we had a special bond. When she and her family moved to Littleton, Colorado, a few years ago, I sobbed uncontrollably. As hard as I tried, I could not stop crying, and today I believe my weeping was the Holy Spirit grieving through me because He knew what the future held.

After Dee moved, she and I called each other at least once a week just to stay in touch and share up-to-date news on our families. On April 20, 1999, we had our usual weekly chat. A short time after we hung up, Dee called me back and asked me to begin to pray, because she had heard there had been a shooting at her son's school. I immediately called our church prayer chain and many others to pray.

That afternoon was torture for me. I tried to reach my

sister, but the circuits were all busy. She did get through to me once and told me that the situation looked even worse; now there were bombs involved! By this time, the news media had picked up on the story and I was able to get some information from television and radio. Later in the afternoon I was able to get through to Dee by phone and the story was still the same. My nephew had not been found.

Hours passed and the reality of what was happening began to hit hard. I had experienced several episodes of extreme anxiety in the past and had even received medication for it. Well, I began to panic, and God suddenly sent a message to my mind: "What did Paul and Silas do when they were chained in prison?" Sing! I knew I had to praise God, so I put in a tape of old hymns and began to sing praises to the Lord. With each song I sang, I felt the fear diminish, and a peace that cannot be explained enveloped me.

Dee called late that evening. She had been at the school waiting for an answer. She was hoping her son would come home but she knew he may have been one of the ones who had been shot. She began to experience extreme weakness and told her husband she couldn't stay at the school any longer. She said she had to go home and as she left, she was hit with an overwhelming sense that her son was one of those killed.

At home, Dee took a shower, thinking it would give her some sort of physical relief, and she cried out to God. She prayed that God would be glorified if, indeed, her son was gone. She called to share all this with me and then a few hours later, the confirmation came. Her son, my dear nephew, had been killed in the library at Columbine High School.

I cannot begin to tell you all the miracles that took place after that. People came to Christ through hearing about the kids that were killed at Columbine. So many testimonies! So many miracles! Even the funerals were filled with God's glory.

Since this tragedy, I have had the opportunity to share my testimony several times and I know of many lives that have come to Christ as a direct result of my nephew's death.

I will never forget the glory God showed me during that time. As a matter of fact, your letter about God's glory came out shortly after the whole incident took place. It was after I read your letter that I received clearer understanding of what I had experienced.

Praise God for His faithfulness, His love, and His rich mercy.

## Our Whole World Collapsed in a Minute

My husband and I had always treasured our three children, two girls and a boy. Although my husband wasn't very vocal about his faith, I knew he was saved. I always took the children to church because their dad didn't want to go, but he shared in their spiritual upbringing in other ways. They all loved the Lord and served Him.

We were a normal, happy family and life was good! We had absolutely no idea of the tragedy that would strike on a warm spring evening. Our son, Dennis, 25, was married and had two small children. He and his family lived very close to us, so we saw them often. His two-year-old daughter went almost everywhere with her daddy and that evening he brought her over to see us. The new baby boy, only five weeks old, stayed home with his mother.

It was a beautiful day, about 80 degrees, and Dennis and little Lindsey joined my husband and me for a bite of supper. Then Dennis told us he was going to go help a friend from work tear down a building. He took Lindsey home and got on his motorcycle for the drive over to his friend's place. He left our place about a quarter to five and twenty minutes later he was dead!

Until that moment, I never knew what it meant to rely on the Lord with every ounce of my being. Our whole world collapsed in a matter of minutes. We were all completely devastated and in deep, deep shock. I felt as if my heart had been ripped out of my chest. Questions bombarded my mind:

How could this have happened?

How are we going to get through these next few days?

How can I look at my son lying in a casket?

How can we go through the rest of our lives and never see Dennis again?

How can we watch our grandchildren grow up without a daddy?

All of these things were almost unbearable to ponder. I knew God said He would never put anything on us that we could not bear, but I thought He surely had made a mistake in our case.

"I can do all things through Christ, who strengthens me." (Philippians 4:13)

"God is my Rock. I can run to Him for safety; He is my shield and my saving strength, my defender and my place of safety." (II Samuel 22:3)

"Look unto the hills from whence comes your help. My help comes from the Lord who made heaven and earth." (Psalm 121:1)

I had known these Scriptures all my life, but now it was time to put them into action. Through all the long days and nights, I didn't think I was going to make it. Well, truthfully, I have to say that I didn't want to make it. I cried out for God to take my life. I simply didn't want to live any longer. It would be easier to be dead than to live with all the pain and grief. I felt like I was hanging on by a thread—but that thread was Jesus Christ!

It was so hard for me to go back to church, since that's where Dennis's funeral had been held. What a blessing our pastor was during this time. Many days when I was home alone and really needed someone to talk with, he would be there knocking on my door, saying, "God sent me to see you today." What a blessing! When I look back now, twelve years later, I realize that God had everything under control all the time. He has each of us in the palm of His hand.

No, these twelve years have not always been easy, but we have to accept the rain with the sunshine. I know for certain that God will take us *through* the storms in our lives, not around them, under them, or over them—just right through the middle sometimes. However, He will be right there with us to shelter us under His wings. Now I can say with certainty that "God is my refuge and strength, an ever present help in trouble."

## "She Didn't Make It, Honey!"

Speeding down the highway well over the posted speed limit, my heart was pounding like a jackhammer and I had a roaring in my ears like a freight train. Completely oblivious to my surroundings, I raced through the night focused entirely on my destination and what awaited me: the emergency room and my daughter.

My wife had called to tell me that our Emily had been in a car accident and, as her dad, I was hurrying to her side to assure her that everything was going to be all right. After all, this is what I had been doing for the last eighteen years. Tearing into the emergency room, I was immediately led to a small room off the main hallway where my wife, Joan, and several doctors met me. I looked at Joan and asked, "Where's Emmie?" She then spoke the words that have ricocheted off my heart ever since: "She didn't make it, honey."

Unthinkable! Our beautiful 18-year-old daughter had been killed instantly by a drunk driver. He had been traveling 70 miles per hour, going north in the southbound lane of a four-lane highway. I felt that I had failed as a father. I had not been able to keep my child from harm, thus I could no longer claim to be the "protector" of my family, the desire of every father.

Our lives were shattered and the days, weeks and months that followed seemed to meld into one blurred time frame. We rode a roller coaster of emotions as we tried to reassemble our lives. My wife and I would go grocery shopping and suddenly feel ill when we spied one of Emily's favorite foods, macaroni and cheese. One day we had to abruptly leave the store because we felt so sick. At other times we would be walking through a local mall and spot a young girl with the exact same hairstyle as Emily's—prompting another immediate exit!

Driving to work I would hear one of Emily's favorite songs and instantly break into tears of immense pain. Even as the months turned into years, the jagged edges of my broken heart would occasionally make me painfully aware of her absence. It was at such times that God's grace came on the scene, wonderful, marvelous, saving grace!

My wife, Emily and I had all three received Christ as Lord and Savior ten years prior to the crash, so we had the comfort of knowing that she was with Jesus. Still, Joan and I had moments of questioning God, often with anger toward Him. How could something like this happen to good, Bible-believing Christians? How could He allow the devil to do this to us? Why hadn't He intervened? He certainly had the power! Could it be that God was punishing us for reasons that only He knew? Why didn't He just tell us what His plans were? WHY DID HE TAKE OUR ONLY CHILD FROM US? SHE WAS ONLY 18!

Six months after Emily was killed, we had a house fire that caused major damage to a portion of the kitchen and master bedroom. It was so severe that we had to move into a hotel for six weeks. Interestingly, an amazing thing took place in us. Instead of being *really* mad at God, we just kind of shrugged and said, "After losing Emily, losing part of the house is just not that big a deal."

Throughout the next year, we had to do battle with the criminal justice system to see that the drunk driver received proper punishment, and our faith sometimes was stretched to the breaking point. Still, no matter what was thrown at us, we seemed to draw closer to God. We became very vocal about drunk driving and the horrendous results it can cause. Speaking at various churches and Safety Council driving classes was good therapy for us, and helped our healing process.

Joan and I had tried for years to have another child and had reached the point of accepting the fact that adoption was our only option. We had been to a local reproductive therapy center for over a year with no positive results. Finally, in February of 1996, after hearing, "Sorry, not this month" once again, we decided enough was enough. Obviously we were just not meant to have another child of our own. Then on March 10, which just happened to be our 24th anniversary, Joan picked up the last of *hundreds* of the home pregnancy tests we had bought through the years and figured she would give it a try. Why not? Miracle of miracles, it turned pink! We couldn't believe it! "We" were pregnant!

After crying and hugging for hours, we realized that no matter how many times man and science say NO, when God says YES, He means YES! In October of 1996, a new baby girl was born into our family. She is a living example of God's eternal grace, and while we know that she was not meant to replace Emily (nobody could ever do that!), we know God sent her to us to love and cherish until we are all together again for our heavenly reunion.

Because of our journey through grief, our church chose us to lead a grief support group for those who have experienced the sudden, devastating loss of a loved one. God's loving strength has carried us through and healed us and we can show others our Lord's grace. We are a testimony that His grace is sufficient and through our "weakness" He has become "strong" in us.

## The Way of the Cross Leads Home

In 1969 my husband and I were a reasonably happy, churchgoing (but unsaved) couple. We had three children, and life seemed quite normal until a heartbreaking day in the spring of that year. Without warning our youngest daughter, Rachel, died and we were completely without comfort. It was truly the darkest day of my life and I went into shock. I suppose shock is a sort of protection to enable you to go forward one step at a time and do what has to be done.

Rachel was a special little girl and seemed to have wisdom beyond her years. She was a leader in her class at school and loved Sunday school and church choir. She had a grasp of God that I didn't have and she liked to talk about Him. Everyone in the neighborhood loved her; in fact, everyone who ever met her loved her!

Our pastor and church did all they knew to do, preparing food, sending flowers and cards, and visiting us. I had never known it was possible to hurt as much as I did. I asked why her, why me and just why, why, why. To compound my suffering, some of my friends were a lot like Job's, passing judgment on me and telling me that God was punishing me by taking our daughter. It didn't make sense, but it added to the pain. We later learned that a flu virus had attacked her heart.

After a long summer and oceans of tears, I was left alone in the house because the other children had to return to school. I was lonely, depressed, and hurting and I wondered if I would ever again be happy. I felt abandoned and no one shared the truth of Jesus with me or prayed with me.

One experience right after Rachel's death impacted us all. My oldest daughter said God's presence came into her room a few days after the funeral. She described this "presence" as the brightest light she had ever seen. A little later I had the same kind of encounter in my living room. I sat lost to the world, wondering where Rachel was and what she was doing, when suddenly across the room a light appeared. It was suspended in mid-air, touching neither the ceiling nor the floor of the room. It's hard to describe the glow, but the room became so bright it seemed like a million light bulbs were on. I was not yet saved, but I knew something spiritual was going on.

A short time later, a lady visited me and gave me a book by T. Austin-Sparks. The book deals with spirit, soul, and body and it inspired me to reach out to the Lord. The author wrote, "In the setting of all of self aside and enthroning Jesus Christ as Lord, the Holy Spirit came." The Holy Spirit quickened those words to my heart and I was born again! God gave me a vision of myself kneeling at the foot of the cross. The cross was in black and white on the printed page and became three-dimensional as I stared at it. With fear and trembling I slowly raised my eyes to the top of the cross and saw that it was empty! Praise God! Right then I received the baptism in the Holy Spirit.

Two weeks later I went to the church we had been attending and God gave me a word of knowledge (a gift of the Spirit) and told me that our pastor was not born again. I left that church because I felt I needed to fully follow after Christ. Sadly, my husband did not want to go on with the Lord and we divorced. I suffered much injustice in the legal system but greed drives people. I had to turn it all over to the Lord and pursue Him and He never failed me.

After my vision of the cross, I began to study the Word of God in order to gain a greater understanding of Jesus and His sacrifice. As the words to the old song go, "The way of the cross leads home; it is sweet to know as we onward go, the way of the cross leads home." Through the years God has been faithful to supply my every need and I have received much, much healing. It is done!

## Youthful Rebellion Leads to Tragedy

I have been married for 25 years and am the mother of three children, two young adults who are married and settled down, and a teenage son. I have been an intercessor for years and the children have heard the truth all their lives. They were dedicated, saved and baptized in a powerful, full-gospel church.

Our youngest, Davie, was always the class clown, smart, witty, almost too quick for his own good. He was an honor student without even trying until about the 8$^{th}$ grade. He is also the youngest of five cousins and we all live close together. Davie spent his days making all the older ones laugh at his antics and proving by his quickness that he could keep up with any of them.

When Davie was 15, his older cousin (who was also his very best friend) started experimenting with drugs. In his immaturity, Davie felt he had to prove he wasn't afraid and he certainly didn't understand the power of heroin. Who really does? They started by sniffing it. Now understand, we are country people, and it is strange to have a flow of heroin through here, but that's what was cheap and "in" at the time.

I'm sure you are well acquainted with the story. His personality changed, he became addicted, and nearly died. In

His mercy, the Lord allowed Davie to be caught by the local authorities and the next thing we knew, we were in court looking at our son in shackles and handcuffs. I had never imagined that I would ever see my beautiful, red-haired, smiling boy looking like that.

I'll leave out lots of details, but I'm sure you can imagine the praying, crying and questioning that went on in our household. I was so mad at Satan for trying to get away with this! (I had always prayed every day for protection for our family, and I pled the blood of Jesus over each member.) We have a free will, though, and sin opens doors to the enemy.

As we prayed and cried, the Lord was silent for three weeks, and this was a new experience for me. Finally, at the end of three weeks, He said one thing to me, "I put the shackles and handcuffs on and you should praise and thank Me." So I did. I had to change my whole perspective and praise the Lord in spite of the pain I was feeling.

God got our boy off the streets and off the drugs, but he sat in an 8' x 8' cell alone on his 16th birthday. Then he was off to rehab. Rehab is a whole different story; Davie ended up with no personality, no joy, no life. This scared me more than the drugs!

When Davie finally finished rehab and went back to high school, he was harshly judged and rejected by everyone. Even the teachers shunned him; any teacher who tried to talk to him or care for him was rebuked by the other teachers. (A faculty member later told me this.) We were forced to take him out of high school, and we got him started working in the family construction business with his dad and older brother.

It was very hard for us to allow our son to become a dropout. It was almost as traumatic as seeing him use heroin. But at this point, we wanted to keep him under our wing 24 hours a day, if possible, so we could observe him and allow him to heal.

Slowly our Davie started to heal and even laugh again. His confidence was extremely low but he worked hard and got in good shape. He stayed with us most of the time and we were all getting back to a place of happiness and ease with each other.

Then the summer came! By the end of June (six months after he completed rehab), weekend parties started. He began to break curfew and he did whatever he wanted on weekends. I had a talk with him and told him that we couldn't parent him anymore—we were turning him over to the Lord and asking Him to be his parent. He replied, "Good! Then stop worrying," and he walked out the door.

I did stop worrying—until about 4 o'clock in the morning on June 9. That's when we got the worst call a parent can get. "This is the Medical Center and your son has been life-lined here." And we thought he was at home in bed! Everyone in the area knows that if you are life-lined to this particular medical center, it's because you either have a serious head trauma or you are near death.

My husband and I rushed to the hospital and found that our son was in surgery to release swelling in his head. He had been in a serious car accident and had been thrown through the driver's side window. His back was broken and his spinal cord traumatized, leaving him paralyzed from the waist down. Even though this was all incredibly hard to accept, the Lord gave grace during that time and many good things have come from this accident. Let me enumerate the blessings:

- Davie had no brain damage, so we have the same son with the same great personality. This was a miracle—lots of prayer had gone up to God.
- He had lost the hearing in his right ear and it returned, thanks to prayer.
- He had to stay in a rehab center (for physical therapy, not

drugs this time!) and learn to live in a wheelchair and take care of himself.

- He is self-sufficient, but still needs us.
- We had to learn to think about a life we had never thought about before: "handicap" everything! We are a hard-working, healthy family, but our focus had to change.
- Davie is home now! He believes the Lord saved his life and has him in the chair in order to slow him down and change his heart and life.
- He completed his GED (high school equivalency studies) easily.
- He is applying for computer programming classes at a local tech school and college.

I have always had childlike faith and known the grace, peace, and blessings of the Lord, but this is a whole new level of knowing God. I never would have known this powerful side of the Lord if our boy had not been tested in this way.

As Davie's parent, I truly trust Christ for him, and look forward to a miraculous future for my son. I know all these hardships will bring glory to God. It is only worth it if lives are saved and changed.

## The Miracle Lives On

After five years of marriage, Mark and Angela had purchased a home and were preparing to welcome their first-born child, a daughter. Everything was going well until the baby began experiencing distress while Angela was in labor. An emergency C-section was performed and the baby seemed fine. However, when she was ten months old, her eyes crossed and she began vomiting severely. A brain scan was quickly performed and it showed a tumor that was one-third the size of her brain.

This kind of news is shocking and hard to grasp, and loved

ones look to the specialists for advice and comfort. However, Mark and Angela were receiving mixed messages. One surgeon said the tumor was so vascular that he wouldn't think of operating because the baby would bleed to death. He wanted nothing to do with the case. Thankfully, another surgeon believed in giving little Nicole a chance.

Immediately the word went out that urgent prayer was needed, and God's people responded. The youth pastor of the family's church called people for a special prayer meeting and not one person declined. One man said that as he prayed, he felt like calling that tumor "into court." He pronounced the tumor guilty of invading the body of Christ, then he cursed it in the name of Jesus.

Another friend was praying and the Lord led her to Psalm 118:17. When she shared this, the church put a variation of the verse on its outside marquee: "Nicole will live and not die, and proclaim the marvelous works of God."

The lead surgeon briefed the family and told them that he planned to remove as much of the tumor as he could. He projected that Nicole would be in surgery at least eight hours, and he took great pains to warn them of possible problems that could arise. For instance, since the surgeons were going through the vision and motor skills portion of the brain, she could have tunnel vision and even paralysis until the swelling went down. But God was moving! Churches all across America were praying for Nicole!

A week after her surgery, her family took her home. Today, at 15, Nicole is an avid reader and a straight "A" student who plays the clarinet and loves the Lord.

God is good!

## "I Can't See! I Can't See!"

When my husband and I were told that our beautiful, sweet, three-year-old daughter, Amanda, was mentally retarded, we were brokenhearted. Five years later, when she was diagnosed with a brain tumor, we were in disbelief. In fact, I was so shocked that I felt like I was going to die. We were a Bible-believing family and it seemed impossible that this was happening to us.

Amanda had surgery on the tumor and it was non-malignant, but for some reason her condition worsened. She cried for an entire month and the doctors didn't seem to be able to do anything for her. Finally they found out that spinal fluid had been leaking into her brain, causing her head to swell, so she went back into the hospital to have this fluid drained. During her second hospitalization, she was in a great deal of pain and she wouldn't eat. She lost so much weight that she looked like a five-year-old.

Our hearts were crushed over and over. My husband would stay at the hospital during the night and I would stay during the day. When I left the hospital, I would cry all the way home and at times I became almost hysterical with grief and anguish. I would fall to my knees and cry out to God, "Why should I serve You? I've given my life to You and look what's happening to my daughter! She's in pain—and I can't help her. Why, God? Why should I serve You?" I was so desperate!

One night I heard a voice (not audible but very clear) say, "You do not serve Me for what I can do for you. You serve Me because you love Me."

My spirit responded, "Yes, Lord, You're right. You don't owe me *anything,* but I owe You *everything.*"

I was hurting so much and needed to hear from God so badly. In His mercy, He spoke to me and my life was changed forever.

Amanda improved and we resumed our normal routine. About six months after her surgery, I was scheduled to give a testimony of the faithfulness of God on a television program. The day before the taping, however, our daughter started to scream, "I can't see! I can't see!" She held her head in her hands trying to ease the excruciating pain. Examinations revealed that she was losing her eyesight! Either the tumor or the pressure from the spinal fluid had caused serious optic nerve damage.

Again, devastation! What was happening? Our church went to prayer right away and God began to move in power. Within three months, Amanda's eyesight began to improve and today she is fine. Migraine headaches, which had plagued her for years, also vanished!

Because of the pressure and strain of my daughter's illness, I fell into such deep depression that I had to be hospitalized for a month. My marriage was falling apart—the whole family was falling apart—and I just wanted to die. But God was with me and brought me out of my terrible state.

God powerfully restored the relationship between my husband and me, and today we have a wonderful marriage. Truly God is the restorer! Amanda will soon celebrate her 20th birthday and she is still progressing well. She will graduate from special education high school this spring and will be moving into a Christian facility sometime next year. With God, all things are possible!

I do not know why we had to suffer so much and go through all that we did, but I have learned one very valuable lesson: trust God, no matter what!

## What Part of "He's Healed" Don't You Understand?

Several years ago our youngest child, Annie, gave birth to her first baby, a precious little boy, Timmy. He was the joy of the family, needless to say, and we all doted on him. From birth, Timmy's skin had a deep tan tone to it, but we thought this was probably due to my Hispanic heritage. When he was eight weeks old, the pediatrician examined him and expressed alarm at what he saw. Subsequent scans confirmed the doctor's fears: Timmy had hydrocephalus, a condition commonly referred to as water on the brain. In spite of our distress and alarm, we immediately started praying, enlisting the prayers of everyone we knew.

Annie and her husband, Justin, went directly to God's Word for solace and wisdom, and they felt that God was going to heal Timmy. I must admit that I wasn't so certain. The medical explanation and prognosis made the situation look so grim that I had a problem considering anything beyond what we could see. The doctor explained that Timmy had suffered a stroke while he was still in the womb, and this had caused a cyst to form at the base of his brain. This cyst blocked the tubes that normally drain fluid from the brain, so he would have to have a shunt surgically implanted to accomplish this drainage. The shunt would run through the cyst, and a tube would then go from the shunt to his abdomen. The fluid would drain into the abdomen and be absorbed by his little body. When I knew there was something they could do, I felt better, and I began to thank God for how He was working. I didn't realize that He had much more in mind for us all.

When I went in to see Timmy after surgery, I was amazed at how different he looked. Before his surgery at eight weeks of age, his head had been the size of a one-year-old but now it was perfectly normal. Also, his skin had changed—he was the color of peaches and cream all over! We were so thankful.

The doctor explained to us that as Timmy grew, he would have to have the shunt replaced occasionally. I was fine with that, but Annie wasn't. "Mom, God has healed Timmy completely and he doesn't need that shunt." I tried to humor her, but in the back of my mind I thought, "Poor Annie, she just hasn't accepted the fact that Timmy will have to have this shunt for the rest of his life." Little did I know at the time that God had different plans.

Annie asked the neurosurgeon if Timmy really would have to have the shunt for life; then she asked a second question. "How can you tell if he doesn't need the shunt anymore?" The doctor replied that the only way they would be able to tell would be to go into the brain—"And that's never going to happen."

Annie and Justin held steady and Timmy seemed perfectly well for about four months, then he developed a fever. The doctor told the parents he had an infection and gave them some antibiotics. Timmy felt better for a time, then the fever returned, and this time he kept getting sicker and sicker. Annie took him to the doctor ten times in one month. One night he got so bad that they took him to the emergency room where it was discovered that the shunt was infected. At 11 o'clock that night, little Timmy had major brain surgery, and the first thing the surgeon did was remove the shunt. The brain fluid should have been clear, but Timmy's was thick and dark, so the doctor replaced the shunt with two drainage tubes on the *outside* of his head. At the end of the tubes were bulb-like containers that the fluid would collect in. Timmy continued to have brain infections and he was put on massive doses of antibiotics. The doctor repeatedly went into his brain to flush it out.

Prayers continued to be lifted up for Timmy's complete healing. My mother, who lives 200 miles from us and attends a small church, had been in constant prayer. One day while Timmy was in for another surgery, a man and woman came into the waiting room and asked for the family of Mary Collins (my mother's name). The room was filled with family and friends and we just looked at each other. Who were these people? We were happy to find out that the man was my mother's pastor, and he and his wife were in town for a wedding. He came to the hospital to tell us that while he was praying for Timmy, God had spoken to him and told him that

Timmy was healed! Such joy filled the room as we gave praise to God!

During Timmy's hospitalization, many events demonstrated God's hand in everything. Only one antibiotic had proven effective against the major infection Timmy had, and for some reason it stopped working for him. We started praying and the very next day the doctor came in and reported, "I don't know how it happened, but some of the other antibiotics seem to be killing that infection we were so concerned about." That good news was followed by a serious challenge, however. He brought in the latest scan results showing that the cyst was full of scar tissue and it would be impossible to put another shunt in unless it collapsed. So *again* we prayed—and the next day we got the news that the cyst had collapsed. Through this experience I learned that God uses doctors to guide us in our praying because they give us specific details.

We went through many such episodes of bad news, more prayer, and then good news. What seemed to be a setback just proved to be another occasion for God to show forth His power and love. What a witness this tiny baby had become in that hospital.

After six weeks of hospitalization, numerous surgeries, grave infections, and unexpected problems, Annie and Justin finally were able to take Timmy home—without a shunt. One night she called me with excitement in her voice, "Mom! Those two tubes just fell out of Timmy's head and he's lying here so peaceful you can't believe it!" She called the doctor to tell him about the tubes and he said, "Well, just leave them out and I'll put them back in later." He never did! Praise God!

Annie took Timmy back for regular check-ups and each time she got the same report: He's doing fine and he doesn't need a shunt! As she left the doctor's office after her last visit, she had to go back in because she had forgotten something. She overheard the head nurse telling someone about

Timmy and she used the word "miracle." Truly God performed a miracle in our grandson.

Timmy is now six years old and he is completely normal in every way. He's an adorable child who rides his motorcycles and four-wheelers, plays basketball, and enjoys all the "boy" things in life.

When you go through something like this and see God answer prayer on a daily basis, it's something you never forget to thank Him for. The memories may fade but the gratitude is constant. Annie has often said to me, "Mom, I don't know why God decided to pour out His grace on us. We are so unworthy, but we are so thankful to Him!" Annie is able to minister to other parents with children who are going through challenging medical problems. She tells them, "Listen to the doctors but don't *believe* them—believe in God!"

I often see people, both Christian and non-Christian, who ask me about Timmy and I tell them, "He's healed!" Many of them answer, "I know, but how's he *really* doing?" I just repeat, "He's healed!" Some get it and some don't.

---

## I Knit You Together in the Womb — You Were Never Hidden From Me

---

If ever a baby was born with the prospect of a gloomy future, it was our son Todd. During my pregnancy, we were told that he had a one-in-ten chance of being severely retarded—if he lived! I had to admit that this dreadful prognosis momentarily knocked me off my feet, but Jesus was right there to pick me up. He spoke to me through the Word: "The Lord your God is with you, He is mighty to save. He will take great delight in you, He will quiet you with His love, He will rejoice over you with singing." (Zeph. 3:17) At that moment I gave our baby to God, even though I was overcome with fear.

I am learning how to fight debilitating fear with the Word of God. I had no idea how I was going to get through the remainder of my pregnancy knowing that the doctors thought our baby was going to be so handicapped, but I prayed and searched the Word and He didn't allow fear to overwhelm me.

When my husband, Darren, and I found out about Todd, we were still recovering from the death of Darren's dad. It had been a tough year but God had sustained us through all that happened. We were looking forward to our baby with a lot of hope and the news we got was such a setback. I can see now that even though last year seemed to be the worst year of our lives, spiritually it was one of the best—because we learned so much about the love of God.

In November our precious Todd was born. We got to hold him for just a moment, then he was taken to the nursery for special care. Because the blood flow into his lungs was inadequate, they stuck together, causing them to collapse. The technical name for his condition is persistent pulmonary hypertension in newborns but we weren't interested in the technical side of things; we just wanted our baby to survive. He was put on a ventilator, and life-saving measures were immediately initiated. We continued to receive dire predictions of what was going to happen to him, but we kept on believing God for a miracle. We had a very sick baby—but God did many wonderful things.

At one time when Todd was not responding well to treatment, I began to thank God for every wire, tube, line, IV, and any other machine he was on. It was not easy, but I was determined to trust God with everything! I found it such a privilege just to be able to change Todd's diaper and watch him fight for life.

I have learned to give thanks to God in every situation because He is good and He works all things to our good. He knows every tear, hurt and fear, and He can handle every situation.

"If God cares so wonderfully for the flowers that are here today and gone tomorrow, won't He surely care for you?" (Matthew 6:30)

"Give all your worries and cares to God, for He cares what happens to you." (I Peter 5:7)

Truly, God is our refuge and strength. We have to learn to trust Him and thank Him, for He *will* give peace that passes all human understanding. There were times when I was strong in God and my eyes were fixed on Him. There were also times when my eyes became fixed on the situation around us and I was not strong at all. During these times I experienced the truth of these words: "I will keep you in perfect peace if you keep your mind steadfast on Me and always trust Me...I am a rock you can always stand on." (Isaiah 26:3,4)

During this time three songs heartened me and gave me courage. "God is Good, All the Time," "Be Strong and Take Courage," and "He Makes All Things Beautiful in His Time." I would alternate singing these songs during the various changes in Todd's condition. All we heard from the doctors was, "It will take time," and I kept singing, "He makes all things beautiful in His time," not giving in to the fear that tried to invade our world.

The Word of God was such a comfort and strength. As I sang and gave thanks to the Lord, I prayed over and over, "No weapon formed against Todd will prosper, and every tongue that rises up in judgment shall be condemned by the blood of Jesus." (Isaiah 54:17)

The doctors told us that even though they were still taking lots of steps to fight for Todd, he seemed to be getting stronger and his "numbers" had stabilized. As I sat by his bed and watched him lying so small and helpless, I could do nothing but trust in the Lord. We weren't allowed to touch him or stimulate him in any way so that he would not waste oxygen by reacting.

After a few days, Darren told God that he was all prayed out and didn't know what else to do. Within a few minutes, he started thinking about Abraham and Isaac and their story found in Genesis 22. The next morning my mother told me that two close family members had been in prayer and all they could think about was Abraham and Isaac! Another mother leaving the ICU stopped me and told me that God had spoken to her about our baby. She hugged me and said, "God says that you're to dry your tears, the victory has already been won." She gave me a little devotional to read—about a newborn baby. It was a sweet story and right in the middle of it was this admonition, "You must place your baby on the altar."

When our pastor came to visit us at the hospital, he said that he had been leading the church in prayer and shared with the people that he felt they should pray that we would *put Todd on the altar!* Well, you can be sure that we got the message. We gave Todd back to God and I continued to place him on the altar because I didn't want to accidentally pick him back up and carry the burden. I was absolutely amazed at the different ways God was getting His message through to us!

A little later in the week Darren was reading to Todd out of the book of Mark and he read the verse that says, "Lord, I believe, but help my unbelief." We made that our prayer and although there were many tears and even moments of fear, through it all God came to us at the perfect time and taught us what He wanted us to learn.

I know fear is not from God; the enemy just waits for an opportunity to come in and attack. Darren and I are learning that there is greater power in God than we ever knew and we are learning how to use our authority in the name of Jesus. The Bible is full of Scripture after Scripture to encourage and strengthen us. This has been an amazing time in our lives and we are so thankful to have our baby. He is a gift from God and we can hardly wait to see what God has planned for his life.

# PART FOUR

# LEARNING
# THROUGH TRIALS

## You're Allergic to the
## Whole Outside World

When my husband, John, and I moved into an "energy efficient" home with our four-year-old son, Joshua, we were excited and grateful. What we didn't realize about this house was that it had a faulty gas heating system that almost destroyed my health. I began experiencing headaches, fatigue, dizziness, and low-grade fever not long after we moved into the house in 1979.

The next year I endured a marathon of visits to doctors and allergy specialists who administered the usual blood tests, x-rays, and medications. After a three-week hospitalization and enrollment in a clinical ecology unit, I received a formal diagnosis of "environmental illness," also known as "20th century allergy." Apparently the carbon monoxide poisoning I suffered in our home destroyed my immune system and caused me to be allergic to virtually "everything in the world" around me.

John and Joshua had not been affected in such a major way because they spent a lot of time outside the home, but I was home all the time. In fact, as I got sicker, I spent almost all my time at home.

Besides being unable to tolerate any fragrances, fumes or synthetics, I was allergic to almost all foods. There were only twelve foods I could eat on a four-day rotation and, frankly, I wasn't very excited about eating any of them. They were odd foods that I had never been exposed to, like millet (a grain), buckwheat, and lots of fish.

For ten years I functioned in a limited manner. At some times I was completely debilitated and couldn't even care for my son. At other times I was able to take care of the basic chores around the house, but not much more. Because of my extreme sensitivity to fragrances, I had to avoid people completely, so I couldn't go out. At one point I spent six entire months totally isolated in one room!

About a year after this last extreme episode of isolation, my husband decided we needed to move to the country, hoping the cleaner air would make me feel better. We actually took our sleeping bags and slept in different areas for up to two weeks at a time—once in a tent and another time in a barn (with the horses). It was a traumatic time, but we were desperate to find a place I could tolerate. We *had* to move because I was practically dead from living in the heavily trafficked area where our home was located.

We found a place to settle down and the move helped me, although I still had to be very careful and limit my contacts with people. I began taking long walks along the country roads where we live. As I established regular walking routes, I made friends along the way. By standing upwind a short distance away, I was able to visit briefly with neighbors and got to know some of them quite well.

One of these new friends was a young mother with three little boys. She was not a Christian—she didn't even attend church—and I longed to share the Lord with her. Remembering how much Joshua had enjoyed Christian cassettes and videos when he was younger, I offered to lend her some of them. I explained that they taught children old-fashioned values like honesty, loyalty, and responsibility. This started a new outreach for me.

This new friend's three boys really enjoyed the videos and as I met new families, I began lending more and more videos and cassette tapes. It was rewarding to see these resources so well received by the mothers when I explained that they taught traditional values. But the best part was the reaction of the children! I love children so much and knowing they watched the videos over and over thrilled me.

This informal lending library is going strong and I have expanded my inventory to include full-length Christian movies as well as children's Christian books and classics. Joshua is now grown and I have extra time on my hands, so I often deliver the materials to the busy mothers. Most of the forty or so families who now borrow the resources are not Christians, so I thank the Lord for opening up this door of witnessing in our area.

I am happy to report that my "first mother" who borrowed the videos is now a born-again Christian. She had been brought up with no religious training at all, but she wanted her children to have some. Now her children attend Sunday school and the entire family attends church. My husband believes that my neighborhood library ministry has been used to bring about true revival.

Had John and I not been Christians when this condition hit me, I honestly do not think we would have been able to stay together. But by God's grace, we happily celebrated our 32nd wedding anniversary recently. Furthermore, I believe that without God, I would either be dead or in a mental institution somewhere. As it is, I have the peace and joy of the Lord!

## Pay Attention!

Several years ago while visiting my parents, I became ill during the night. Since I have a very high pain threshold, I ignored my symptoms and didn't awaken my husband, as I should have. In fact, God had nudged me awake earlier in the night and said, "Have your husband take you to the hospital because your appendix is rupturing." To this day I can't figure out why I didn't believe that it was the Lord speaking to me. I think I figured that if it was really God telling me I had a problem, He could just HEAL me. How ignorant of me!

We had to catch a flight back home in the morning, so I went ahead and got on the plane with my family. And on the flight my appendix ruptured! The plane made an emergency landing and I was rushed to a hospital for immediate surgery. I have very little memory of that week in the hospital, but I do remember that I was very ill and thought I was dying. The doctor kept telling me I was fine, but I certainly didn't feel fine.

One day while lying in the hospital bed sleeping (or maybe I wasn't really sleeping), I felt the most awesome presence I have ever known. I actually felt like God was holding me and telling me it was not over, and not to be afraid. He said for me to trust HIM. He said they were going to be telling me that I would die, but I was not to believe them, for He was in control. All I had to do was believe Him! For a moment I thought it was a dream, but it wasn't. I have never again experienced such perfect peace.

I was released from the hospital and after only 12 hours I had to be re-admitted. They discovered an abscess and I was kept in the hospital for four days before being allowed to go on home to my personal doctor. When my personal physician saw me, he admitted me to a local hospital. He told my husband that he didn't think they could keep me alive through the night. What was going on?

The abscess really needed to be removed, but my body had already started to shut down and I was too weak to have the surgery done at that time. I had such a supernatural peace. My pastor, family, and friends kept asking me if I was afraid, and I kept replying, "NO! I know what He told me—He said this would happen, and I am not going to die."

When I was able to have surgery, it was a success, although I lost some of my small intestine. I spent a month in the hospital and several more months recovering. But God was faithful!

Many times I ask myself why things had to happen the way they did. In my case, I feel I had to go through this because I did not listen and obey the first time He spoke to me. God was not allowing me to be punished, by any means, but I did have to suffer the consequences of not waking my husband and doing the thing God said to do. He still could have healed me, although He used the doctors. But He allowed me to live, even though the doctors themselves didn't think I would. They actually said they did not think I would survive, but the Lord is gracious because He loves His children.

God has blessed our family, and several times down through the years He has saved me from death. I don't understand why it happens to some and not to others, but I do know that HE is in control. I trust Him to care for me and my family and no one could ever convince me that He is not real. There are not enough words to say how wonderful He is.

## Wisdom Sweeter Than Honey

Seeking God can sometimes bring disfavor rather than

favor, as was evidenced by several of us a few years ago. Three friends and I felt a great hunger to know the Father better, so we met together on a regular basis to pray and fellowship around His Word. We were surprised and upset to receive a letter from our ungodly pastor asking us to leave the church.

Oh, how badly that hurt! Here we were, crying out for truth and seeking Him, and even our pastor would not support our search. My husband reminded me that just before his mother died, she had told him he should get a Hebrew study Bible like the one she had. This was a great idea and I ordered one right away.

I studied key words in the Hebrew (as well as Greek) lexicon, and found additional meanings that opened up my understanding. As I studied, I got a clearer, broader meaning of God's Word, and found out that sometimes our English interpretation isn't quite complete. Discovering this Bible was like finding a light at the end of a long, dark tunnel.

A little over a year ago, my brother succumbed to a rare form of leukemia. He was the baby of our family and his death hurt us all a lot. I continued seeking God and taking nourishment from His Word. I found key Scriptures to hang onto for strength and He kept me steady.

My dad had Alzheimer's disease and had to be put in a nursing home. This is always a difficult decision, but it was necessary in his case. Sadly, a member of the nursing home staff pushed him and he broke his hip. After surgery, his condition deteriorated and about three months later he died. My husband and I had been attending a new church, but because we were not yet members, we were denied certain privileges during this time, which compounded our pain and sense of loss.

I realize that hard things happen to everyone in one way or another, but when one blow lands on top of another, and then another, the pain can cause confusion. I took my questions and uncertainties to the Lord and asked for truth—His truth! I came to realize that He allows us to go through adversity in order to cause us to depend on Him at all times, in every circumstance. No exceptions!

The Scriptures are my source of comfort and wisdom. He gives me revelation knowledge that is sweeter than honey and I praise His holy name!

## A New Baby — A New Mother

My children are home schooled and my ten-year-old daughter repeatedly asks me why she wasn't born already knowing everything. Life would sure be easier! Well, my answer to her is that this is what separates people. If we were all born knowing the same things, we would all be just the same. It is up to her to strive for knowledge in the academic world as well as in her understanding of life.

I feel that God has shown me the same thing for my life in the spiritual sense. Many times I had asked Him why He wouldn't just reveal all His truths to me right away (without the trials!) and He reminded me of what I tell my daughter. If I seek, I will find. How hard am I willing to work for knowledge of Him? The more precious and valuable His truth is, the more willing I should be to work hard to obtain it. I keep asking myself if I am truly willing to forsake everything for the prize of knowing Him. Am I willing to abandon everything for that great pearl?

Well, God heard my cry, and when my hard trial came, I discovered that I didn't personally *know* the One *I knew so much about.* I had been diagnosed with a kidney problem but I pretty much ignored it, because I didn't want to admit that something could be wrong with me. Besides, I didn't have any obvious symptoms. However, when I became pregnant with my third child, my life changed forever. We had two children we deeply loved, but they were a lot of work and I didn't really want any more. This third baby was a big surprise and, frankly, not a pleasant one. I was terribly sick the first three months and I thought that was a big enough trial, but it got a thousand times worse almost overnight.

By the fourth month of my pregnancy, I was swollen almost beyond recognition. I did not look pregnant, but obese! My normal weight of 125 pounds ballooned to 175 and I can tell you, I just wanted to die. I was physically sick, but I was also disgusted with my appearance. The swelling didn't seem to be that big a deal to some people, but to me it was appalling. Before my pregnancy, I was vainer than a peacock because I thought I looked pretty good. I was probably a stumbling block to many, because I was very flirtatious with men, even in my church. This weight gain was the most humiliating thing that had ever happened to me in my entire life (in my opinion). Truly God was dealing with my pride!

To make matters worse, we were attending a church that taught that when I wasn't healed right away, it was because I didn't have enough faith. A very close friend said to me, "Why are you putting up with that? If that were me, I would pray for God to heal me." I *was* praying for God to heal me and that incident makes me very cautious about how I judge others and what I say to them. That was an important lesson for me.

Because of my kidney condition, I was sent to a specialist who deals with this type of pregnancy. She informed my husband and me of all the things that could go wrong if I chose to "continue my pregnancy." She pointed out the possibility of retardation, premature labor, and severe permanent damage to my kidneys. Abortion was absolutely not a consideration for us, but afterwards I became very depressed. I was put on total bed rest for the duration of my pregnancy. I was so miserable that at times I secretly wanted to miscarry. I was so selfish that I wanted to know the earliest possible date the doctor could safely take the baby—even if he had to stay in the hospital for several months. Looking back, I cannot believe that person was me! Thank God, He had another plan and I realize how far He has brought me.

At first, I was angry with God because He didn't heal me. I had always faithfully paid my tithes and now I thought it was time for payback from Him. (How presumptuous of me!) After realizing that my swelling was not going to go down through diet, I began to look in the Bible for healing. I didn't fully realize it at first, but I was not seeking God, I was merely seeking healing. I am happy to report that while I was seeking healing, however, *I found God.* I saw that the Word did not fully line up with the doctrine I had been taught and I realized that I didn't truly know my Father. I had felt guilty because I thought I was doing something wrong, and I was very torn. But in all my "knowing about" Him, I had missed knowing Him. Since I had nothing to do all day but read, I began searching anew for Him.

One day I asked God why He was allowing all these bad things to happen to me if He really loved me. Mercifully, God showed me something to answer my question. I awoke in the middle of the night with an indescribable feeling of the presence of God and He showed me an example of His "parent love." He allowed me to "see" my daughter in great pain and I also felt incredible pain as I observed her. With every fiber of my being, I wanted to end her suffering, and I knew that I would have taken her pain in an instant if it were possible. This only lasted for a few moments, but I interpreted this to mean that God was showing me the pain He feels when we suffer. I know some people may think I just conjured this up in my imagination, but my reaction was so entirely contrary to my usual selfish mindset that I knew it was God.

God brought to mind the consequences of King David's

sin with Bathsheba. The Bible says God struck their child and David pleaded with God for his life. I had always been taught that anything bad that happened was from the devil. Was that just Old Testament teaching? Or, if God is the same yesterday, today, and forever, could He still be disciplining His children today? What about the husband and wife that were struck dead for lying to the Holy Spirit in the New Testament?

I remembered the people in the New Testament who did things in His name, casting out devils and healing the sick, and He still said, "Depart from Me, I never knew you." If those people healed the sick and cast out devils and still didn't really know Him, then where did that leave me? They were real individuals and they must have thought they were going to heaven. I wasn't doing any of those things—and this made me question whether I really knew Him, either.

God was giving me a lot to think about, and He was tearing my doctrine apart. I began to realize that I had to be torn down before He could build me back up, because I needed a new foundation. God was using this time to change my life in a drastic, dramatic way, and I'm happy to say *it worked!*

There is a happy ending to this testimony and this is my favorite part! When I got close to my due date, my blood pressure started to elevate. It looked like the doctor would have to induce labor but I wanted to go the natural route. When contractions started, I went to the hospital and the doctor ordered the nurse to start the "pit drip" right away (the drug pitocin stimulates contractions). I asked him to give me thirty more minutes before he started it, and he reluctantly agreed. To everyone's surprise, our baby boy was born 37 minutes later—without any medication!

Thanks to a miracle from God, our baby was healthy and strong, defying all predictions and expectations. The delivery room was filled with neonatal specialists to take care of a number of possible problems that they thought may arise, but they were not necessary. The baby was perfect! How good God is! I felt like He was smiling on me and saying, "You passed this test and I am pleased with you." What a great feeling!

Needless to say, this "surprise" baby is very special to our family. It was through him that God changed my life forever. In fact, through him I learned to love my other two children like God intended. I am a different woman, a different mother, a different wife. I don't even know the woman I was before. I know from experience that God can change anyone! I also know He is faithful to complete the work He has begun in me. Praise His name!

## My Focus Changed from Earth to Heaven

Ten years ago I had some very vague symptoms that were finally diagnosed as a connective tissue disease called scleroderma. This disease strikes all the tissue in the body, and eventually an over-production of collagen blocks blood vessels in almost all the organs. In my case, this resulted in congestive heart failure and thickened walls in my lungs, which blocked the flow of blood to the rest of my body.

My fingers became hard as stone, and my joints and skin hurt, like I had the flu. Fatigue and weakness plague me daily, but difficulty in swallowing and stomach upsets have not yet hindered my appetite. After this elusive disease has been diagnosed, high fatality rates are common; in fact, I lost three friends in a support group.

Because of allergic reactions to medications, I could not become a test case, and the doctor warned that I would not live through a heart/lung transplant, which I need. Very little research is being conducted on this disease, and there is no known cause or cure. Why continue with doctors? The Lord is my hope and my enduring source.

After receiving my diagnosis, I went straight to the Lord. I was a little numb and in a state of shock. "Lord, what do You want of me at this time? What am I supposed to do?" I cried out to Him through my tears, and in His still, small voice, He questioned my heart in return. "Will you love and follow Me and also serve Me even if healing isn't immediate? Will you trust Me and use the disease to encourage others who are in dire circumstances?" It didn't take long for me to give Him my unconditional YES.

I recognized my need to dig more deeply into the Word, and as the Lord began to teach me, I saw many of the blessings He had provided for me. My husband, Reed, has been faithful to our wedding vows "in sickness and in health," and he has the heart of a true caregiver. I praise God for this gift.

As a means of building myself up, I began writing letters from my heart to Jesus, expressing my devotion to Him. His Word became more powerful in me as I wrote, and after about six months, He impressed on my heart to send letters to others in need. Soon, I was writing monthly letters and these grew into a ministry of encouragement. Instead of concentrating on myself, I was allowing Him to do a work in me that focused on others.

In 1995, my lungs became harder and I had a major heart attack that left my heart damaged. So today, on oxygen, somewhat isolated and separated from activities, I continue to write and send letters to over fifty women. I had always longed for more time for intercession and He has granted my heart's desire. Scleroderma doesn't receive much of my attention, praise God. The nature of Christ and the power of the Holy Spirit is at work through me. Glory!

Two years ago I was told I have about five years to live but I don't dwell on that, or the weakness and pain. Actually, my mind is focused on things above and not on the earth beneath. My medication is the Word of God. My help in time of need, my hope and joy are all centered in Christ. He speaks to me daily and carries me through by His Word.

"But as for me, I trust in You, O Lord; I say, 'You are my God.' My times are in Your hand." (Psalm 31:14,15) Nothing goes unnoticed by Him, so I let Him plan my days.

"...Yet who knows whether you have come to the kingdom for such a time as this?" (Esther 4:14) God has given me purpose, here and now!

"This is the day that the Lord has made; we will rejoice and be glad in it." (Psalm 118:24) Rejoicing reduces overwhelming difficulty.

God didn't promise life without struggle—this brings us into faith in Him. In fact, Jesus said, "In the world you will have tribulations; but be of good cheer, I have overcome the world." (John 16:33) We gain victory through trial, triumph in battle. Darkness cannot be avoided while we're on this earth, but belief in Christ leads us into an overcoming provision for winning the war, finding help in time of need, and strength for each day.

"I can do all things through Christ who strengthens me." (Philippians 4:13)

"The Lord gives strength to His people; the Lord blesses His people with peace." (Psalm 29:11)

What is my part in all this? I rest in Him—surrender— yield to all His blessings! This way I can walk in victory.

## There Really Are Happy Endings

Sitting at the kitchen table fighting back panic, I reached for the mail and saw your newsletter. I tore it open and read your pointed and most welcome admonition to trust God, no matter how things look. Immediately "the light went on" and I realized that I was just going through a test—and God was in control!

I called my daughter and in a calm voice I was able to remind her that what had just happened was going to be resolved in God's way. What *had* just happened? Well, Tessa had called to tell me that someone had answered an ad to buy her car. She let the girl test drive it and she just kept on driving! When the girl didn't return, Tessa called me and that's when panic hit and fear gripped our hearts. It was hard for Tessa to comprehend that someone would do something like that. Furthermore, she and her husband could not afford the loss of several thousand dollars.

When I reminded her of the words you wrote in your newsletter, and the perfect timing of my receiving it in the mail, we both relaxed, assured that God would resolve the matter. Then she and her husband began to pray for the thief.

In the course of time, the insurance company paid for the car. Then the car was found in a ditch and the girl went to jail. Tessa felt that the Lord would be pleased if she contacted the girl and witnessed to her about Jesus.

This is just the most recent event in my life that has brought me face to face with a loving Father. In 1979 I was divorced and left alone with three small children. My family was completely torn apart, and I was so overcome with pain and fear that it was about six years before I could function properly. At one of my lowest points, I heard God tell me that He would be my husband, so I committed my life to Him. I really didn't have any idea if that meant I would be alone for the rest of my life or not, but I wanted to be in His complete will. I needed His strength.

I was able to buy a dumpy little house, remodel it, and

finally pay it off. The Lord found me a good job at a university, where I worked for 14 years before retiring last year, with enough income to be comfortable. And best of all, my children are doing very well now, and all three are serving the Lord.

All through the years, I have been faithful to tithe from the firstfruits, to give liberally to missions and other ministries, and serve in my church. I have fallen many times, but my focus has been on Jesus and He has been the joy of my life. I thank Him daily for His faithfulness and His many blessings. I was quite settled and satisfied with my life and had no idea that God had plans to "unsettle" me quite abruptly.

Early one December morning, my phone rang and I assumed it was a telemarketer. To my surprise, it was a former classmate of mine whose wife had recently died. He was on his way through town to visit his daughter and wondered if he could stop by and see me. Thus, the whirlwind began!

Bill and I had gone to grade school on the same school bus and graduated from high school together. Then our lives went in completely different directions. When he called that morning, then came by for a visit, we fell into a comfortable, easy time of getting reacquainted. Soon we realized that God was bringing us back together for more than friendship, and the long distance phone calls started getting longer and longer. The happy ending of this story is that Bill proposed marriage—and I gladly accepted! He will retire from his lucrative construction business this year, then he will come to the area I now live in and build a house—a home—for us.

God has given us a relationship that is wonderful and precious, and we are content and full of joy at His goodness. It is still hard for me to take in all that He has done and the treasure He has given me. Truly, this is "exceedingly above all I could have asked or thought" those many years ago. I am so thankful that He enabled me to remain faithful to Him.

## God, I Don't Want Grace, I Want Things Changed

My parents were a typical post-World War II couple. Dad, a Navy man, and Mom both graduated from college and started their life together with high hopes. They joined a large church, had two daughters, and settled into a nice, comfortable middle-class life. Things went smoothly until 1957, when adversity hit our family in a life-changing way.

My mother, a lovely, efficient woman, contracted spinal meningitis and encephalitis, and from then until the day she died in early 2001, her life was a struggle. The extremely high fevers left her with memory loss, *petit mal* seizures and excruciating headaches. Also, her personality completely changed, and this was very unsettling for my sister, Beth, and me. Mom was a different person and as time went on, we never knew if she would pick us up after school or if she would forget about us. We left notes everywhere for her and drew maps of how to get places. Only after I had children of my own did I realize how terrifying this must have been for her—to have children and not remember where they were, or even how old they were.

Mom's terrible headaches continued and she would take painkillers, then take more because she forgot she had taken them earlier. Dad called several times every day to check on her and when he didn't get an answer, he would rush home to find her passed out from too much medication. The strain on my father began to wear him down, but both my parents held the family together with their faith in God. Mom spent lots of time reading her well-worn Bible, and at night Daddy would gather us all together and read the Word to us. Often he would strum his baritone ukulele and sing Beth and me to sleep with songs that included "'Tis So Sweet to Trust in Jesus" and "What a Friend We Have in Jesus." This was a great testimony to us!

Along with all this difficulty at home, Dad took care of my mother's aging parents. After my grandfather died, we built an extra room in our house and took my grandmother in to live with us. This created a difficult situation, because Mom could hardly remember her old, familiar surroundings and routine, much less a new one. Stress built up between Mom and Dad as Grandma's health worsened and there were emergency runs to the hospital with her. We girls could feel the tension but there wasn't much we could do to help, although we tried.

On top of all this, my parents were not satisfied with the teachings at our church, so they eventually left and found a smaller one which they felt followed the Scriptures better. Another change, another stress, yes. But my parents were founded on the Rock even when the storms beat hard against the shore.

In 1968, I went off to college and was glad to be out of the confusion and all the stress at home. I wanted the freedom to explore my own interests. However, the situation at home rapidly deteriorated and Mom got much worse. I didn't realize how much she had counted on me to "remember things" and do them. My sister never knew what she would find when she got home, and because she couldn't handle it, she began to drink heavily. Then she got into drugs.

Dad had a heart attack in 1970 and although he recovered, his heart was damaged and he was unable to do all the physical things he had done before. But he could still pray! And as he and Mom watched Beth get worse and worse, they stepped up their prayers.

A year or so later Beth came home one night and announced that she had been saved and baptized in the Holy Spirit—and she could speak in tongues! This was all new to my parents; in fact, they had never heard anything like it. But they could see a change in Beth! She started reading her Bible all the time and when I came home from college, I found a different sister. Actually, I was shocked when I saw the transformation. My parents didn't understand it all, but they knew God was answering their prayers. Before long I was also baptized in the Holy Spirit, as were both my parents.

My parents began hosting home meetings and we were all growing in the Lord. It would be nice to be able to say that everything got better and we lived happily ever after—but instead, we were just in the calm before the *big* storm.

In 1972, my mother had a stroke and, amazingly, she recovered and her headaches were gone. What a blessing! Mom was like a new person and she and Dad had a wonderful year together. Beth was able to have Mom help her plan her wedding and they developed a closeness that they had never had. It looked as if God had poured out His blessings on our family at last—we had come through the storm!

Then in 1973, two days after my sister's wedding, Mom had another stroke and it was very debilitating. She was almost completely paralyzed and unable to talk. At first we all were sure that God was going to miraculously heal her. So many people prayed for her! We even took her to big healing meetings, but she wasn't healed. By this time I was through college and living with my parents to help care for Mom.

Mom's care was very demanding, both physically and emotionally. It was also very time-consuming. For instance, we had to cut her food into tiny pieces, then slowly feed her. Also, she had to be given fluids to drink many times during the day. We hired help for the daytime, when Dad and I worked (I was now a school teacher), but we would share the afternoon and night shifts. We were able to communicate with Mom by having her squeeze our hands and through her facial expressions.

Years passed—many years. Twenty-eight long years! Think about that—28 years of being a prisoner in your own body, hoping someone will think to ask you if you need a certain thing, hoping someone will think to tell you what you want to know. Years of not being able to turn over, or scratch, or wipe a tear from your eye. There were many trips to the hospital for broken bones, infections, removal of objects lodged in her throat, and other such mishaps. The list goes on and on.

During those years I met a wonderful man who moved into my parents' home after our marriage and helped care for Mom. We were blessed with four lovely children and we were a happy family. However, the constant trials continued. When Mom was hospitalized, a family member had to be with her at all times because the staff was not prepared to care for someone who could not communicate or feed herself. We knew Mom's habits and what to be cautious of. For instance, we had to be sure no one put a thermometer in her mouth because she would involuntarily bite it into pieces.

Pressure mounted in the home and at times things got quite difficult. My husband and I worked hard at keeping our relationship strong and the one thing that kept us together was Jesus. He gave us grace for each situation as it came along.

We home schooled our children and at times I even had my sister's two children (she also had to be hospitalized for a time). One day I looked around: Here I was, home schooling four children, chasing after my toddler, and caring for my infant. And still taking care of my parents! I don't know how I did it—but God poured out His grace and not only gave me strength, but made it fun! I felt that I was handling every-thing pretty well—never imagining that another fiery trial was coming.

In 1989, our youngest daughter was diagnosed with a malignant tumor in her right orbital bone that required sur-gery and chemotherapy. Then the month after her treatments ended, my father was diagnosed with congestive heart failure and given six months to a year to live. Mom's condition was deteriorating and I felt like I was about to fold.

Sometime during that period, God and I had a heart-to-heart talk and I told Him I was just tired of everything. Things just kept coming at us and it didn't seem fair. He continued to pour out His grace, but I finally told Him I was tired of having grace—I wanted the situation changed! Did I ever learn a lesson! God removed the grace and it took less than a day for me to get on my knees asking for forgiveness for my lack of trust. I realized I *needed* His grace and I knew that it was truly sufficient for any situation.

There have been many, many other trials and I know other people go through some of the same things we faced. Some of the most difficult tests were the small, day-to-day things, the things people don't see. This is where the grace of God is most important. When there are obvious crises, people are there for support; they acknowledge your trouble, they are concerned, and they pray for you. But the inner struggles, the hidden heartache can go on for years. These are the things that are just between God and us. No one else understands; no one else even sees them. This is where God's grace is most evident to me.

People have a tendency to praise me for taking care of my parents, but they don't see the whole picture. They don't know the inadequacy I have felt, the helplessness, and they would never conceive of the anger I have dealt with. Daily irritations, the small, unimportant things, build into major obstacles as they are repeated day after day. That's where God's grace really is abundant. Daily grace! His mercies are new every morning!

Dad had always wanted to live longer than Mom so that he could care for her, but that was not God's plan. He went to be with the Lord in October of 2000, and Mom followed him three months later. One of the last things my father said to me before he died was, "I persevered. Not everyone does." Without a doubt, it was God's grace that enabled Daddy to persevere through years of trials and disappointments. And it was God's grace that enabled him to finish the race.

Mom and Dad lived pretty much hidden from the outside world and people who knew them were either blessed or troubled by their situation, depending on their perspective. Some did not understand how my parents survived, and they were frightened to think about it because they were afraid something like that could happen to them. But those with open hearts and minds saw a testimony to God's grace in the midst of great suffering. This is the grace that is available to each one of us!

## A Second Chance

My wife, Jeanie, and I were camping in the mountains where we had just purchased forty acres of alpine forest. Busily building a cabin that we had dubbed our "home away from home," we were realizing a lifelong dream. Truly we were getting our piece of the American pie.

We were in the truck driving down the mountain to get some supplies and do laundry when "it" hit. Blood vessels in my esophagus ruptured and I began to lose blood rapidly. This massive hemorrhage made me so weak that I stopped the truck and crawled into the back to recline on an air mattress while Jeanie drove me to the nearest hospital. I could barely drag myself into the emergency room, and the personnel ascertained immediately that, truly, I was in crisis. They treated me and later I was flown by air ambulance to a large, metropolitan hospital.

The physician who treated me determined that I was in liver failure. He told us the shocking diagnosis, then declared that my condition was "terminal." Jeanie and I held each other as we wept, and we felt there was nothing to do except resign ourselves to the inevitable. The doctors told us they could do nothing but help me manage the pain.

Within three months my weight went from 196 pounds to 138, and I felt even worse than I looked. My abdomen filled with fluid and the pain was almost unbearable. To add to my distress, nausea and vertigo were my constant companions.

I took care of my business affairs and prepared for my funeral. Jeanie and I looked through the casket catalog, arranged the details of the memorial service, purchased a double grave lot with a grave marker, and gave lots of hugs to family and friends. My pain became so severe that I actually looked forward to dying, so I committed my soul and body to God—and waited!

In an attempt to help me deal with the pain, the physicians did exploratory surgery. In desperation, two of them stood at my bedside and prayed for wisdom. Soon after their prayers, my head physician came in and told me he had thought of a doctor in a larger hospital who was doing some interesting, experimental things with liver patients.

"Would you be willing to see her?" he asked. Of course, I would. After all, I had nothing to lose.

The next day, after being transferred to this new hospital, I immediately slipped into a coma, stopped breathing, and was placed on life-support systems. I was no longer able to even breathe on my own.

My name was placed on the waiting list for liver transplants and three days later I underwent the nine-hour transplant surgery that saved my life. The medical team told me that I could not have survived an additional two hours, even with life-support. That was in 1992.

I had a difficult and slow recovery, but I learned to face life on different terms—one hour at a time. My body was so wasted that I had to re-learn to walk and feed myself. Everything I did was a challenge. I had so much medication pumped into my body that it was impossible to keep my mind focused. At one time, I had hallucinations for three straight days and nights and I thought I had undergone brain surgery. My whole world was goofy! Some of the things I imagined were rather comical. I thought the doctors were high school students and the nurses were housekeeping personnel. One night I heard the city garbage truck emptying the dumpster eleven floors below and I tried to get out of bed so I could take the elevator down and hitch a ride on the truck. My intention was to ride to the nearest hamburger joint and get a hamburger, along with fries and a bowl of chili. My appetite was returning with a vengeance—but the nurse discovered my plan to escape and promptly tied my hands and feet to the bed!

Two weeks after surgery, I was dismissed from the hospital. My son came to drive me home and my first request was a stop at McDonald's for a hamburger. He graciously complied and my taste buds were delighted. However, when I unwrapped the burger and attempted to take the first wonderful bite, I was unable to bite through the meat—I was that weak! But that was a small matter. I was free from the needles, tubes, bedpans, sleep interruptions, and many other inconveniences of hospital life, and I was a happy camper. I was suddenly filled with such joy that I burst into tears and wept all the way home—from sheer happiness and amazement that I was still alive.

How does one express to God one's gratitude for the gift of life? Or to the organ donor and the family of the donor? Or to the surgeons and medical team? Or to the many friends and church groups that prayed? Thank you, thank you, thank you!

Since my transplant surgery in 1992, I have had some other health problems, but God has proven His faithfulness to me over and over. Today I am enjoying better health than I have experienced in a long time.

Trials and troubles are universal and we all have days when our world shrinks to the narrowness of our own concerns. The big issue is, how do we respond to our trials? We have heard the saying, "Hard times will either make us *better* or *bitter*." It is in the crucible of suffering and in that long, dark night of the soul that one comes to grips with the basic issues of life. Once those issues are resolved, difficulties are no longer the criteria by which we judge life.

As I reflect on the past few years, I am happy to share a few recommendations for those facing trying times:

1. Embrace your family; they are your best support system and you will need them on your journey.
2. Check your priorities. Be prepared spiritually for whatever happens.
3. Cherish your friends. Their loving support is one of your most valuable assets. Right after you hug your family, hug your friends.
4. Recognize the absolute irrelevance of most material things. A big house, car, and bank account are not of much value when you are dying.
5. "Don't sweat the small stuff." Don't turn minor things into major issues, because fretting and worrying are the opposite of trusting. Being frustrated over things that are beyond your control is a waste of precious time and energy.
6. Don't ever stop "walking your faith." Place your life and your case in God's hands, then rest! If you lose hope and faith, you lose two of the essential ingredients in the healing process.

It is not enough to simply "put a geranium in your 'at and be 'appy." Neither is there a verse of Scripture that says, "Grin and bear it." There is, however, a verse that says, "Whenever trouble comes your way, let it be an opportunity for joy. For when your faith is tested, your endurance has a chance to grow. So let it grow, for when your endurance is fully developed, you will be strong in character and ready for anything."

## God, Is This Some Kind of Sick Joke?

When I was sixteen, my dad was diagnosed with chronic leukemia. He was advised to have a bone marrow transplant and his brother turned out to be the perfect match. But even with the transplant, Dad survived only thirteen months after his diagnosis. As my dad lay dying, I was able to spend lots of time with him, and as he took his last breath, the song playing on the radio was so appropriate: "Think about His love, think about His goodness." In spite of many, many prayers for healing, God took my dad home for his perfect healing. Our lives were changed forever, of course. My mom, who was a homemaker at the time, had to start working to make a living, so she got her degree in nursing and has been able to help others who have needed her.

Five years after my dad died, I planned to get married. I chose my two brothers, one older and one younger, to give me away at the wedding. It wasn't the same as having Dad there, but it was sweet. Just a few months after our wedding, I received a phone call at work telling me that my younger brother had been in a serious car accident. I drove two hours to where he had been air lifted and the doctors told us he wouldn't survive 24 hours. He had a massive brain injury and had stroked out on each side of his brain. After an agonizing few hours, the family decided to take him off all life support equipment. To everyone's surprise, he survived!

Survival means different things in different situations.

Even though my brother is alive, he merely exists. The neurologist told us that he doesn't believe my brother has enough brain left to have any coherent thoughts. He lies in a nursing home in a vegetative state, unaware of his whereabouts. He is fed through a tube, has no speech, is paralyzed on one side of his body, and makes no eye contact. He is now in his twenties and "healthy" and he may live to be 80. My poor mother sees her son lying there day after day not responding to anything, and we miss him so terribly. It's torture to know he'll never change except for a miracle from the hand of God.

We know now that the path my brother was following before his accident was one of drugs, alcohol, theft, and destruction. One of his closest friends at the time of the accident was just recently indicted for first degree murder and we realize my brother might have been in that drug-deal-gone-bad. We have many questions about why God allowed this to happen to my brother, but we have learned to rest in His wisdom. He is sovereign!

As we all know, life goes on, and my husband and I agreed that it was time for us to have a child; however, we were having some problems. In fact, we were having serious problems. We went for infertility consultations and found that I had some severe physical abnormalities. We attended a revival service and when the pastor invited people up for prayer, we went forward. We didn't tell the pastor that we were having any problems, but halfway through his prayer, he asked, "Do you want children?" We just stared at him with questioning eyes. "Well, God is impressing on my heart that you are going to have them!"

My husband and I began to weep because this was the encouragement we needed to hear after all our prayers. We went home in a state of bliss, knowing that God was going to give us our miracle baby sometime in the future.

It was over a year before I got pregnant, but our hopes

were dashed when I had a miscarriage. I reacted emotionally and started inwardly screaming at God, "Is this some kind of sick joke?" I have to admit that it took quite some time for me to recover spiritually. In a few months, though, I started the fertility medication again and everything went well for a time.

Our joy knew no bounds when we found out I was carrying twins! We were so thrilled—but then I had to have emergency surgery and these babies were also lost. We could hardly believe it, but this time I handled the loss quite differently. I believe I had matured a lot since my former miscarriage. I went through a time of grieving naturally for my children, but I didn't get angry at God for "taking my babies."

After this last trauma, I had to heal physically before getting pregnant again. During this time I fell into a pit of despair, one I hope I never return to. Several factors entered into this depression: I felt like a failure as a "mommy" because a mother's first priority is to protect her children; I felt guilty because I couldn't give my husband children; and I didn't feel like I would ever feel the kick of an unborn child inside me. The "problems" just built up to the point where I gave up and we started the adoption process.

While our names sat on a list for adoptions, we also continued to try to have a baby on our own. By this time my medical condition was quite complex and I worked closely with the fertility personnel month after month. It really would take a miracle for me to get pregnant again—but I did! Mixed with the exhilaration, however, was a lot of anxiety. Every little cramp or twinge would throw me into near panic, but my husband and I would pray and find His peace.

This pregnancy was different (or was I the one who was different?) and I sensed an overwhelming awareness of the presence of the Holy Spirit. I knew everything was in His hands, and no matter what happened, I would be fine. As time progressed, we heard our baby's heartbeat—this was a first! And I felt the baby kick—another first! The pregnancy progressed normally and I not only went full-term but I was three days overdue when our living, breathing miracle from God was born.

My husband and I wept as we held our precious newborn son in our arms. We rejoiced with thanksgiving and told everyone who would listen that our son was a miracle from God. We now have "children"—children in heaven with my dad—and a wonderful toddler to keep an eye on. He fills our lives with more joy than we could imagine and we know that we have a testimony of God's grace sleeping in our arms.

I firmly believe that my journey has led me down paths that have caused me to become stronger and more sympathetic toward others. I also believe that all that happened was in God's plan to draw me closer to Him, and along the way I learned to lean on Him and trust Him wholeheartedly. Losing my dad, "losing" my brother, and losing my children were painful occurrences, but I know that He used it all to shape my character. I love my Lord in a new way and I know that He is my personal Friend!

## You Asked Me to Show My *Power* — I Wanted to Show My *Grace*

On my 17th birthday in 1971, I casually stopped in at a local auditorium in Ketchikan, Alaska, to hear a visiting evangelist. I had no idea what was drawing me to the place, but I'm so thankful I followed my gut feeling, because my life was changed!

My heart was full of fear, I was lonely, and anxiety and feelings of inferiority controlled me. I had been reared as a bastard child and I felt resentment just for *being*. On top of this, I was the object of years of abuse and I now know that only Jesus could have salvaged my life. I answered the call to come to Christ at that youth crusade and my life became a miracle.

Brother David, I am part of your legacy! I know there are multiplied thousands who can say that, but here is my own personal testimony.

In 1992, I was afflicted with severe tinnitus (ringing in the ears) and hyperacusis (hypersensitivity to sound). The ringing is a continuous, extremely high-pitched scream (up to approximately 80 decibels). In addition to this, I have intolerance to any external sound that exceeds 40 decibels in volume. Exposure to external sounds that exceed this level of tolerance causes great pain, and exacerbates the tinnitus to a level that increases in volume and pitch for hours, even days.

When this affliction first came upon me, I went for six days and nights without rest, finally caving in emotionally and physically. I suffered a nervous breakdown and lived with an oppressive spirit of suicide for over 18 months. During those first dark days, the suffering and overwhelming anxiety were so great that I wondered if I could still be in my right mind.

There was no place of escape! Every waking moment of my life was tormented by the ungodly noise created in my head by a dysfunction of the middle ear. I had to be drugged at night in order to get any rest at all, and every morning I awoke to the same living nightmare that had become my life.

During these days, God visited my heart in very simple but profound ways. I pored over the Scripture, searching for words to support my hopes of deliverance. I became aware of an all-encompassing truth that was profound in its simplicity: From one day to the next, God's Word never changes! It was the same each day I went to Him and I knew that His words to me would *never pass away.* Oh, the precious, sustaining, immutable Word of God! I lived on His promises, such as "For no matter how many promises God has made, they are 'Yes' in Christ." (II Corinthians 1:20)

While I was working as an illustrator for a Christian organization in Europe, God provided a perfect helpmate for me. Natalie would prove tougher and more resilient than I could have ever dreamed. We went through some desperate hours together. I would come home at the end of the day beyond the point of exhaustion and my dear wife would spend hours standing behind me with her hands on my head, trying somehow to relieve the torment raging in me. She would quietly pray in tongues and her tears literally bathed my face at times.

I have to admit that at one time it seemed the only way out for me was suicide. I just couldn't take it anymore! However, as I cried out, the Spirit of God overwhelmed me with a word straight from His heart and that word has sustained me to this very hour. God asked me to view the scene of the crucifixion from a human perspective. Naturally, from the point of view of His disciples, things looked absolutely *out of control.* I could understand that perspective. But then God began to show me what that moment in history looked like from *His* point of view. For all time and eternity, His master plan for redeeming the human race and drawing mankind to Himself was being completed.

Somehow the truth of God's own word to my heart enabled me to trust Him—no matter how things looked from my finite perception. Things may look completely out of control, but when our lives are in God's hands, He is at work and *He can be trusted.*

Nearly nine years after the onset of this terrible condition on that awful day, I am living one day at a time, by the grace of Almighty God. Through this long, dark, deep valley of the soul, I have found fellowship with the Lord Jesus in the midst of suffering. Through it all, He has tempered my spirit to be intensely sensitive to the needs of those around me who are suffering.

Whenever I pray for the needs of others who are in pain, whether emotionally or physically, or both, it is with the compassion of the Lord Jesus and not my own. He has given me the ability to so identify with the pain of others who are suffering that it comes over me like a mantle. The burden becomes very real and my intercessions are deeper than anything I could have experienced had I not first felt God's hand upon the "socket of my hip."

A dear missionary friend of ours wrote a beautiful poem about grace for me:

### TAKE ME FROM THE FURNACE

"Take me from the furnace, Lord, that all the world may see
Your power to deliver, to set the captive free.
"Open another door," I cried, "and lead me safely through,
So I can give all who ask the hope I've found in You."
In all my anxious pleading He answered not a word,
But in the stillness of my heart, this is what I heard:
"In the furnace of affliction you thought I hid My face;
You asked Me to show My power—
I wanted to show My grace."

Agnes Rodli

(Used by permission)

---

## My Efforts Were Futile — Then Jesus Came!

Cancer took my father's life last year, but there was joy intermingled with the sorrow. My sister and I were able to pray with him to receive Jesus into his heart just *two days* before he died. For 79 years he had walked in sin, selfishly serving himself, but we know he is in heaven now!

I have been a believer in Jesus for 26 years; I wish I could say that I've been a faithful servant, but I haven't. In fact, I wasted a lot of years. My husband and I will celebrate our 25th anniversary soon and there has been a lot of pain in our marriage. I feel sad as I reflect on our early years together and see where we are now.

My husband, William, shared the Lord with me when we first met and I was receptive to the message of salvation. We were married in the Lord and walked together in Him for several years. Then shortly after our second child was born, William confessed to me that he had been having an affair during my pregnancy. Even though there was a child born of this illicit union, my husband agreed to work on restoring our marriage.

William and I continued with our lives the best way we could but over the next several years, alcohol became a big problem for him. Two years after our third child was born, I arranged an intervention for him where he was confronted by several people about his drinking. He agreed to go into a 30-day treatment center and did quite well. When he was released, he appeared to be eager to work at maintaining his sobriety.

During the next few years, we quit going to church regularly because our church wanted to deal so harshly with William because of his alcoholism. They recommended that he be brought before the entire congregation of the church and excommunicated. Rather than stay in the church, we just left. While I now see that this was not the wisest choice we could have made, at the time it seemed our best option.

We muddled through life doing the best we could. One day our two oldest children expressed a desire to attend a Christian, church-affiliated school. We found out that if they attended the school, they were expected to attend Sunday services at the church. We let the children enroll in the school, but we didn't get involved in the church the way we should have.

William gradually returned to alcohol—and this time he added drugs to his routine of abuse. I discovered that he had even stolen prescription medicine from one of our sons. To make things worse, I learned that he was addicted to pornography over the internet and through magazines. As I made these discoveries, I became more and more desperate. I finally realized that everything I had been doing was failing—my efforts were futile. What a devastating realization! I was groping my way through a maze of misery and hitting one wall after another.

Then Jesus came! As William and I approach 25 years together, I can say with certainty that Jesus is the center of my life and I have faith for William's complete deliverance. Through a set of circumstances ordained by God, I have come to know Jesus in a new way. He has required me to die to self and I regret that I lost the last 25 years in selfish living, thinking I could handle everything.

Through my painful situation, Jesus has taken me back to His cross. He has shown me the purpose of His suffering, His obedience, His forgiveness, and His reconciliation. This revelation has liberated me from trying to change what I have no control over. I have been liberated and enabled to intercede for my husband on a daily basis. I contend for his deliverance and freedom from sin because I know that God loves him more than I do and He has plans for him. God's ways are perfect.

I used to complain and judge my husband, but the Lord has enabled me to pray for him with power and confidence. No more whining! My boast is in Jesus Christ and His blood. He holds the power in my life—my joys and sorrows. He pours His grace immeasurably in and over all that I am, and He gives me hope that defies explanation—hope and faith that William will soon come to Him and become the man of God he was designed to be.

## My Quest Is Over —
## I *Know* He Heals Today

Is Jesus *really* the same yesterday, today, and forever? Does He still heal people as He did when He walked here on earth? These questions and others haunted me for years after my father and mother both died within a short time of each other, leaving me an orphan when I was a small boy. I wasn't afraid to query God, "Why did You do this to me? Why didn't You heal my parents?" I knew that my mother had been anointed and prayed for many times, but she died three years after the onset of her cancer.

My uncertainty regarding the reality of faith and divine healing took a back seat as I grew up, and I didn't really confront the issue until much later in my life. In His mercy, God used a sequence of events to restore my faith in Him and helped me realize without a doubt that Jesus is our Great Physician—today!

Our son was born with a double cleft lip and a cleft palate and I became acutely aware of our need for God's healing power. Within weeks of his birth, surgeons began a series of operations to correct the defects. The surgery to close his upper lip was uneventful, but there were complications with the surgery on his palate. It didn't close properly and it looked like another operation was inevitable. My wife felt particularly burdened to pray for our son and I agreed in prayer with her. Miraculously the hole in his palate closed and no further surgery was needed!

A few years later a near tragedy occurred that severely tested our faith and brought us to a point of total dependence upon God. Our younger daughter was struck by a car and critically injured. Agonizing hours of waiting turned into long, seemingly endless days, and I realized my complete helplessness. I could do nothing but pray for her and trust God to spare her life and restore her to health. The entire family prayed earnestly, and our pastor anointed her with oil and joined us in prayer. I received the assurance that God had heard and answered our petitions. She recovered completely and we gave Him all the praise and glory.

We had no way of knowing that our journey of testing would continue and involve every member of our family. I was the next one to face a dramatic challenge. I developed bacterial endocarditis, an inflammation of the membranes lining the heart, and had to be hospitalized. My doctors told me that even with the very best medical care and the administration of life-saving antibiotics, I would most likely have permanent damage to my heart. But those were not God's plans for me! Through the prayers of my loved ones and saints in the church, I was totally healed. Subsequent examinations have found no heart damage whatsoever. I soon returned to work and have lived a normal, active life for the past twenty-six years.

Another daughter was twelve years of age when she began exhibiting disturbing physical symptoms. Through the months, she lost nearly all coordination and had difficulty walking. Eventually she could no longer feed or dress herself and was almost totally crippled. We took her to several doctors, including a prominent neurosurgeon who was a family friend, but all tests were inconclusive. Preliminary findings indicated she was suffering from either a brain tumor or a progressive brain and neurological disease. But if so, which disease?

She was scheduled for exploratory brain surgery to try to determine the cause of her physical deterioration. A week or so before she was to enter the hospital, we gathered at home for our regular evening family worship. I read in John 4:46-54 about the second miracle of Jesus, the healing of the nobleman's son. Before we knelt in prayer, I thought, "Now, if Jesus could heal this man's child, could He not do the same for my child?" I shared my thought with the rest of the family and they agreed.

My daughter asked the family to pray for her and I anointed her with oil. The entire family gathered around and placed their hands on her head as we prayed for Jesus to touch and heal her body. Afterward, she told us she felt a sensation like a powerful electric shock passing through her entire body. We noticed an immediate change in her—a direct answer to our prayer. She grew stronger daily and her muscular coordination improved. The doctors were amazed at the miraculous change that had occurred and cancelled the scheduled operation. After a few months, my daughter was completely normal and there has been no further evidence of the disease—whatever it was! Today she is married and is the mother of four healthy boys.

My wife was the last member of our family to suffer a nearly fatal illness that struck suddenly and without warning. She had an attack of abdominal pain so severe that she was immobilized, and began vomiting blood. At the hospital, the doctors discovered a perforated stomach ulcer and immediate surgery was required to save her life. The first night after her surgery, the children and I knelt in prayer at home and asked the Lord to heal her and help her recover quickly.

When I visited my wife the following day, she told me about an unusual experience she had had the previous night. As she lay in her darkened room, she noticed a small light, much like a candle flame, hovering at the foot of her bed. As she watched, it slowly passed diagonally above her body, lingering briefly over her, and then it moved on to the head of the bed, where it disappeared. She said that as it passed over her, she felt a warm sensation in her body. I knew that as the children and I were kneeling in prayer, the Spirit of God was ministering to my wife with His healing power.

In retrospect, it is so easy to see the hand of God in each of these incidents. I gladly admit that these were hard lessons, but I have tried to learn well. No longer will I ever doubt that *Jesus is the same today* as He ever was. *My quest is over!* I now know for sure that He heals and our family is living proof of God's power to heal all manner of sickness and disease.

The beautiful verses by the psalmist David are my testimony:

"Bless the Lord, O my soul: and all that is within me,
Bless his holy name. Bless the Lord, O my soul,
And forget not all his benefits:
Who forgiveth all thine iniquities;
Who healeth all thy diseases;
Who redeemeth thy life from destruction;
Who crowneth thee with lovingkindness
and tender mercies;
Who satisfieth thy mouth with good things;
So that thy youth is renewed like the eagle's."

(Psalm 103:1-5)

# PART FIVE

# MINISTERING TO AND CARING FOR OTHERS

## Three Hours a Night for Three Nights = A Miracle!

Twenty-five years ago I worked in the emergency room at a large medical center in Los Angeles. I was young, my mother had just died, and I was trying to just get through my shift at work. I worked the "swing shift," which is from 3 P.M. to 11:30 P.M. One evening a woman came up to my workstation and told me her brother, an in-patient, was in a coma and was expected to die that night. She lived in another state and had to head home right away to take care of another urgent family matter. What she really wanted was to sign "body release" forms for her brother so that when he died, his body could be released to the family without anyone having to come back to California.

I referred this lady to the appropriate place to get the help she needed, but before she left, I asked her about her brother.

She told me that his name was Bob Scott; he was in his early 40's and dying of cancer. He was married but had been separated from his wife for many years, and he had not seen his two teenage daughters since they were very small.

I could identify with this family's situation. Not only had my mother just died suddenly from a heart attack at the age of 53, my father had died from a cerebral hemorrhage at the age of 36 when I was only six. To make my empathy complete, my 17-year-old sister had died from cancer when I was 16. This made me very sensitive to this man's condition.

Bob's sister told me that he had no family in the area, so I asked her if she would like my friend, Jenny, and me to spend time with him so he wouldn't be alone. She was happy that we would do this and gave us her permission. With that, she left. This was a Friday night.

Jenny and I had been having our own Bible study on our breaks, so we always took our Bibles to work. This Friday night on our late break, around 10 o'clock, we went up to meet Bob. He was in a coma, so naturally we did not speak to him, but we prayed for him and left. In Matthew 18:19, Jesus says, "Again I say to you, that if two of you agree on earth concerning anything that they ask, it will be done for them by My father in heaven." We decided we would take God at His Word—literally—so for the first time in my life, I asked God for the miraculous. We asked Him to bring Bob out of his coma so we could speak to him. After praying, we went to find Bob's doctors.

I had worked at this hospital for several years and I knew almost all the doctors. When we found Bob's doctor, he told us that he had been in a coma for a day or so and, indeed, was expected to die that night. Jenny and I went back to work and when our shift was over, we went back up to Bob's room. This time when we walked in, Bob was out of his coma. We were so excited! We introduced ourselves to him and told him how we had met his sister. He had that "death look" about him, which I easily recognized because of my hospital experience and the loss of my family members.

Jenny and I stayed with Bob for three hours, mostly just sitting with him and stroking his forehead, arms, and hands. He was clearly in pain, and touch was comforting. When we left his room to go home, we asked God for more. We asked Jesus to "reveal Bob's heart condition" to us because we wanted to know whether he was saved or not.

The next day, Saturday, Jenny and I could hardly wait to get to work. We didn't know if Bob would be alive or not, and if alive, whether he would be alert. And further, if alert, would he reveal what was in his heart? We ended up going to work two hours early so we could spend some time with him if he was still alive. When we walked into Bob's room, there he was, alive and alert! Jenny and I began to share with him that Jesus loved him and cared about his life-threatening situation. Bob immediately revealed his heart's condition by saying that he did not believe what we said about Jesus! We continued to reassure him and asked him if he cared if we prayed for him and read to him out of the Bible. He gave his consent. When we left to go to work, we asked the Lord, "Please, Lord, keep him alive long enough for us to be sure he hears the gospel and has a chance to accept Jesus as his Savior."

We went up to see him on each of our breaks, just to sit with him. After work we went into Bob's room and stayed for the next three hours. We shared the gospel with him as clearly as we could. We constantly reassured him of God's love for him and His concern for his physical condition. Bob was nice about it, but he kept telling us that he did not believe it. After leaving to go home that night, we asked the Lord to let us know if Bob got saved. We acknowledged that we did not *need* to know, but we would *like* to know.

On Sunday we again went to work two hours early to sit with Bob and reassure him that God loved him. We spent both our breaks and lunchtime with him, and after work we went up to spend our usual three hours with him. When we walked into his room this time, he reached out and took hold of our hands, one hand of each of us as we stood on opposite sides of his bed. After he kissed the back of our hands, he said, "Anytime two young girls will spend this kind of time with a man they don't know, it must be true. God must love me—and I accept Jesus as my Savior."

After Bob spoke those words, several things happened. For one, the pain left him and an expression of indescribable peace came over his face. What appeared to be a "halo of light" surrounded his head; in retrospect, I believe this was the Shekinah glory of God as Bob prepared to enter His presence. Bob slipped back into his coma, never to come out of it again. Needless to say, Jenny and I were ecstatic! We sobbed tears of joy at being privileged to witness the rebirth of a soul. We stayed our usual three hours, but anticipating Bob's passing, we asked the Lord this one more thing. We told the Lord that we would stay an additional twenty minutes (why we chose that length of time I do not know) and that if He was going to take Bob home, would He please allow us to be there. God gave us what we had asked—twenty minutes later, Bob died.

The next day I went back up to the ward and shared with one of the ward nurses, a Christian. When I told her that Bob got saved, she was amazed. I learned two things from this nurse. She told me that Bob had refused to let the Protestant chaplain, the Catholic priest, or any other religious staff come near his room. Obviously, God knew that it would take a common person that Bob would not reject to reach him. I am so glad He chose Jenny and me! I also learned that in those three days, *no one* had seen Bob out of his coma except the two of us.

A couple of days later as I was reflecting on the loss of my mother and how God had saved Bob, I had my devotions. The little booklet I chose to read was all about how God can take a time of personal tragedy and turn it into enormous victory. I was so blessed! I knew I would see my mother again someday, and God had comforted me in a way I would never have expected. He had turned my sorrow into incredible joy!

A few days later I copied Bob's sister's address off his chart and wrote to her. I gave her the detailed moments of our time with her brother, sharing his salvation and the fact that we would see him again in heaven. She wrote back and told me that her brother had been angry with God for many years, and was very cynical. She thanked us and I thought that was the end of it.

Ten years later as I was combing my hair in an employees' lounge, a woman whom I did not recognize walked in. When she looked at me, she said, "I know you. You're one of the girls that spent all that time with Bob Scott before he died!" It turned out that this was a nurse who had been working during the last days of Bob's life. She told me that the entire staff was affected by the fact that Jenny and I had willingly spent so much time with Bob. I do not know the extent of the work God did in those three days, or whose life He touched, but someday I will know—probably in heaven.

From this experience I came to realize several things about God:

- He honors His Word
- He honors those who seek Him and His will
- He honors obedience
- He comforts His own (remember, I was still grieving the loss of my mom)
- He is faithful to the end to reach those who will accept His offer of salvation.

Most of all, I realized that as long as there is breath in a man, there is hope! How can I help but praise the LORD!

## This Must Be What Purgatory Is Like

In 1993 I was in my early forties and leading what I considered a meaningful, balanced life. When I felt myself drawn to prayer, meditation, and reading, I realized that I was put on this earth for a purpose other than living a self-directed, self-centered life. I recognized that I was being awakened to spirituality and one day I asked Jesus to come into my life. I understood that anything that came into my life after that time was according to God's will and would be for my better good.

That year I met a man who turned out to be perfect for me, although neither of us was "looking" for a mate. During the months of our courtship, we made weekend trips to a small town near the Texas Gulf Coast looking for a home. We both felt that we would be living near the water, and when we found a tiny, white brick house built in the 1950's, we bought it. I left my big-city, high-tech job and landed secretarial work in our new "hometown" and Alan retired with half pay from his job. Then we got married and moved.

Our life was simple and fulfilling. While I was at work, Alan took care of the house, did yard work, and cooked the meals. We got a great buy on a boat and spent every possible moment fishing. I discovered I was born to fish!!

About a year later we found that it takes only a moment to alter a life forever! On a cool, November Monday evening, Alan and I were watching Monday Night Football—one of our favorite pastimes. Alan was a big fan of the Dallas Cowboys and I was a "Packer Backer." After the game, we retired for the night with no premonition of what was about to happen. Around 4 o'clock that morning, my husband of only 13 months suffered a massive stroke. Thus began our journey into desperation and faith.

The ambulance took Alan to our local hospital and I could tell by watching the staff that he was in serious trouble. I heard the word "stroke" but even though I had certainly heard the word before, I had no idea what it actually meant. Very quickly Alan was transferred to a hospital in a large, metropolitan area. In the predawn darkness, I filled the car with gas and packed a small bag in case he was kept overnight. One of our fishing buddies drove the car for me as we followed the ambulance to the hospital. Alan was rushed to the Intensive Care Unit as soon as we arrived and I began the "long wait."

I believe faith in God's leadership makes traumatic experiences felt more completely because of two definite things: While the active mind deals with circumstances and their ramifications, the inner mind struggles to keep the connection with God uppermost and strong. The "maybe overnight" turned into days and on my third day of camping out in the ICU waiting room, short on sleep, needing a shower, and wearing wrinkled clothes, my soul wailed, "Lord, how can my will and Your will be so far apart? Alan can no longer speak, and his blood pressure is still not stabilized. You know I have loved You with all my heart! Help me!" For the first time since Alan's stroke, I broke down and cried.

A woman in the waiting room recognized my anguish and snatched me up. Although she had been keeping a 24-hour-a-day vigil for her husband, she saw my need and sprung into action. I'm 5'8" and Yolanda is barely 5'2" but she pretty much carried me downstairs to the chapel. She prostrated herself before the altar and prayed for me—when I could not. She reaffirmed my faith in God and in humankind. I will never, ever forget Yolanda! She lived nearby, so she brought me some of her clothes, and then she took mine home and washed them for me. I had no idea at the time that I would be needing my clothes *and hers*.

Alan's blood pressured stabilized, so they transferred him to the critical care floor. Confused and unfocused, he no longer looked like himself. Eyes that were helpless and frightened peered out of a face that struggled to communicate one-word concepts. During the next two weeks on the critical care floor, the word I heard most often was "brow." He constantly begged for a cool washcloth to be placed on his forehead. He was disoriented, his right side was paralyzed, and his vision was severely impaired. Unable to move, he wore diapers. Unable to eat, he was spoon-fed, usually by me. And because he couldn't feel the right side of his mouth, he was a mess.

The next nine weeks were filled with misery, because many negative things piled up in addition to Alan's health crisis. When Alan was transferred to the rehabilitation floor, I left the hospital for the first time since his stroke. Sobbing from the depths of his being, Alan begged me not to leave him, and because of brain damage, he couldn't understand that I needed to get back to my job. All he knew was that he was going to be alone and unprotected, because I was abandoning him. He had no concept of time and couldn't comprehend that I would be back on the weekend. I felt like I was going to die with pain—I wept all the way home.

My weekly routine became a picture of purgatory in my mind. On Thursday nights I would gas up the car and pack a suitcase so that I would be prepared to head for the hospital immediately after work on Friday. I spent the weekends with Alan, catching what little sleep I could in a window seat in his room. I'd wash his clothes and share every minute of his day with him until Sunday evening. Then came the sobbing departure and the two-hour drive back home. I soon became totally exhausted.

Eventually Alan learned to establish balance, although learning to sit was difficult because his brain did not acknowledge that his body had a right side. He was taught to raise his head, which hung so far down that his chin touched his chest. He had to be taught to make eye contact. In his simple state, he got used to wearing diapers, so "potty training" was next in the long process of rehabilitation. Then there were the tasks of basic hygiene. Combing his hair became a project and was helped along with notes taped to his mirror: "Pick up the comb. Comb BOTH sides of your hair. Put the comb back down!" Even with the notes, he would look straight into the mirror and comb only the hair on the left side of his head. *It could get so frustrating.*

As Alan's discharge drew near, I was urged to find a nursing home for him. I found out that his insurance would not cover the expense—and that's when desperation set in. I suddenly realized that I would be bringing Alan home and there wouldn't be the safety and structure of the hospital environment. I was on my own—with the enormous responsibility of being the sole source of Alan's care and well-being. I sold the boat to help defray medical expenses and brought my husband home in late January.

Our neighbor, a retired military physician's assistant, took over Alan's care during the day so I could work. You cannot imagine how much time must be invested in something as simple as hygiene, and February, March, April and May swirled by in a blur. Believe me, I developed a deep empathy for caregivers. Bathing, dressing, and grooming a 275-pound man took a lot of strength and time. Then there was the care of the house and yard, preparing meals, doing dishes and laundry, emptying garbage, and holding down a full-time job. I got very close to the breaking point.

Friends were faithful in giving me books. I prayed. I submitted. I got very little sleep because Alan woke me several times each night with small needs. He really didn't have any concept of anyone's needs but his own. He had convulsion-like episodes at night and one night he vomited in bed. But always, the next morning I would get him up and clean, dress, and feed him—then I was off to work again.

It broke my heart to watch my husband lose everything by which he defined himself. He battled depression over his physical condition, and his state of confusion further dulled his ability to understand and cope with his new status. In May I quit my job; I had lost 25 pounds and was physically, mentally, emotionally, and spiritually drained.

I got two part-time jobs and life developed a routine that was a little easier for me. I learned to stop struggling and trying so desperately to get things back to the way they had once been. Alan and I had lost so much and I had to accept it and search for the good. Part of his brain had been destroyed—I couldn't heal it. His body was disabled—I couldn't fix it. The relationship we had bet our lives on no longer existed—I couldn't bring it back. Our financial plans were out the window and I could not hold on to our dreams.

It does no good to worry about emotional loss, mental loss, physical loss, financial loss, material loss, and loss of friends. I discovered a deeper love and sense of service, a humbling of self in order to focus on another, and an amazing sense of oneness with my spouse. I also developed a greater love and respect, not for what once was, but for what now is. And there is such a rich sense of peace.

For four years my routine went something like this: Awaken Alan each morning with a smile and a joke. Help him sit, then stand, so I can change his clothing. Wash his face, shampoo his hair, feed him a good breakfast, and dispense medications. Then help him with personal hygiene, put toothpaste on his toothbrush, and check to be sure he turns on the faucet. Clean his eyeglasses, settle him in front of the TV, and go to work.

At home in the evening we would discuss the antics of the Deputy of Disaster on The Andy Griffith Show. We battled wits on "Jeopardy," even though he was delighted because he had watched the same program earlier in the day on a different channel and knew all the answers. He knew that I knew his little "secret" and it was all part of the game for him. Here was the routine: Make dinner, do the dishes, help him into bed, rub his leg and arm with lotion, curl up beside him, and read him to sleep. Finally I would turn off the lights, slip to the back of the house and replenish myself through prayer, reading, and thought. And give thanks.

In the summer of 2000, Alan developed chest pain and was hospitalized for two weeks. His digestive tract stopped working and he was diagnosed with diabetes; he had another stroke—and he was dying. I brought him home under hospice care. While he was able to talk, he told me he felt God's presence. I asked him "Where?" and he patted his chest. I asked him what God feels like and he answered, "Nice, fluttery, like butterflies." I asked him if he could see God and he said, "No, but I can see my father and stepmother." They had died in 1999. When I asked him what they were doing, he replied, "They're waiting for me."

His breathing became shallow and slow. He looked like an angel to me, and shortly before he died, I became aware that I was being filled up with an overwhelming sense of joy. When Alan took his last breath, I felt the room lighten. It was an odd sensation, but I could still sense his presence, so I talked to him. Then I felt that he and the "lightness" were gone.

In the months since my husband's death, I have been busy re-ordering the details of my life and following God's leading. Do I still believe that all things lead to good, according to God's purpose? I can answer with a resounding YES. It is a blessing to know the difference between understanding with my mind and understanding with my heart, between loving from my head and loving from my heart. There are times I feel overwhelmed with grief, yes, but more often I focus on the truth of "absent from the body, present with the Lord." And I give thanks.

## Schizophrenia Stole My Son

In 1985, my 16-year-old son, Jeffrey, began to change in ways that completely puzzled those who knew him. He had always been a pleasant, well-mannered, fun-loving boy with lots of friends, and seemingly overnight he became reclusive. He stopped studying and reading and didn't want to leave the house after he got home from school in the afternoons.

Jeffrey's teachers and counselors at school had no idea what was wrong with him; hence, they didn't know how to deal with him. They told me that if I didn't allow him to quit school, they were going to expel him on the grounds that he was incorrigible. Incorrigible? I wanted to know what he was doing to warrant this label. Well, he wasn't doing anything wrong—he was just doing *nothing* and they needed to make room for a student who would study. So what choice did I have? I took him out of school. After he was finally diagnosed, I came to understand that his illness eradicated his ability to read and spell.

How terrible it is to see your child deteriorate right before your eyes! I didn't have an inkling of what to do for Jeffrey and at first I honestly thought he was being rebellious. He became more uncommunicative, almost sullen, and retreated into his private world. He became increasingly worse as time went by and I became more and more alarmed. I *now* know that he was showing all the classic signs of schizophrenia, but I didn't know it then. After all, I had no experience with such things.

A few years ago, schizophrenia was classified as *a disease of the brain* and it is the most common form of psychotic illness. It affects the thoughts, concentration, and speech of the person suffering with it. Symptoms include hallucinations, delusions, hearing voices, and paranoia. Usually the person cannot keep a job even if he is able to get hired.

For two years my family tried everything we knew to help Jeffrey, but when he was 18, he suffered a delusion that forced us to hospitalize him. That's when we finally got a diagnosis for him, as well: schizophrenia-paranoia.

Watching my beloved son suffer from this brain disease caused me to go through several stages of grief:

1. **Blame someone**: I questioned God! I told Him, "Father, when Jeffrey was born, I thanked You that he was not 'mentally challenged' and now, eighteen years later, he has a brain disease. He can't reason; he can't tell what's real and what's not; and he is unable to maintain friend-ships. Why would You let me think he was okay at birth and now we learn that he's not okay?"

2. **Blame myself**: I kept telling myself that I must have done something wrong in bringing him up. Research shows that parents do not do anything during child rearing to cause schizophrenia.

3. **Guilt**: "Why does Jeffrey have to be like this? Here I am, able to think, work, and deal with life. I feel so guilty that he has to suffer this awful illness and I don't have to suf-fer."

My thoughts tormented me. I would wonder, "Why did God tell us in II Timothy 1:7 that He has given us a sound mind? My son doesn't have a 'sound mind' so is this in op-position to the Scriptures?"

Many days at work I would think of Jeffrey and cry, think-ing, "It's almost like the real person is dead because he has lost his personality and mental abilities. He's no longer the same person."

Through the years of my son's illness, some people may have thought, "Oh, her faith just isn't strong enough in the Lord." I sometimes felt that's what they were thinking. But I found that faith grows day by day as we experience the trials of life. My faith grew stronger and I became more patient and serene as time went by.

The Lord allowed several things to happen in my life that showed me how He was in complete control of everything.

1. I looked for a job for almost two years and was surprised that I couldn't find one. I had always been able to find a job rather quickly. After I was hired at a school of nursing, I could see the hand of God at work in keeping certain jobs closed to me and guiding me to this one. He wanted me in this particular setting so that I could receive help when I learned of Jeffrey's illness. I worked as a secretary for the professors at the school, highly educated Christians who encouraged me. They often came by my office to share their knowledge or to testify and they helped me see that bad things also happen to other Christians. It made me feel less alone in my grief and struggle.

2. The Lord led me to a Christian counselor who helped me see things from a Christian perspective. When my insurance would no longer pay for me to see this counselor, he continued to see me without charge—further demonstrating to me the love of Christ.

3. The Lord helped me grow through the Christian books I read. He led me to specific books in a second-hand store.

4. The Lord led me to a woman close to my age who became my friend. Her son was suffering from a mental illness and was charged with a felony that he committed during an episode of hallucination. The judge did not even consider his brain disease and gave him a life sentence. She and her husband now have a prison ministry through their church. Their son's disease has not affected his reasoning and his sense of reality, so he witnesses to prisoners. When one gets saved or is open to hearing more about salvation, he sends the prisoner's name to his mother. She finds someone to write or disciple the prisoner, and over forty inmates have been saved through her son's witness.

My friend and her husband write to inmates and visit several every other week. I now write to fifteen Christian prisoners and send them Christian books, Bible studies which I have written, and Christian articles. I also pray for them regularly.

I have found that during trials it helps to put our grief and anger into something constructive, so that's what my friend and I are doing. I feel that this is one way the Lord has taught me to cope. She and I also encourage one another.

A couple of years ago, Jeffrey was hallucinating and stabbed a person eleven times, once in the face. He now faces a trial by jury and, if convicted, he could go to prison for twenty years. Every time the trial date comes up, the jail psychiatrist diagnoses him as incompetent to stand trial and he is sent to a state mental hospital with maximum security. They have the necessary funding to give him the medication he needs, and when the medication works, he passes the competency test and is sent back to jail. There is not enough funding in the jail system to give him medication, so he is sent back to the hospital. This is the way it goes, back and forth, up and down, and it keeps us all in emotional turmoil.

I face each day trusting in God's grace in this time of testing and suffering and He is so faithful! I also trust God that He will reveal Himself to Jeffrey in ways that only He can! And I continue to praise Him.

# PART SIX

# DEATH OF LOVED ONES

## Jesus Accompanies a Young Jewish Man on His Final Journey

In early January of 1997, I received a telephone call from my son, Adam, telling me he was having severe pain in his upper stomach and chest. He thought it might be a heart attack, so he was rushed to the emergency room. After several hours of tests, doctors dismissed him because his heart seemed fine. However, they warned him that his sugar count was alarmingly high. Since Adam was a diabetic, I also scolded him for not paying proper attention to his sugar intake. Little did we know that the pain and high sugar count were symptoms of the malignancy that would take his life.

Within two months, Adam's pain had increased so much that he went back for more tests. Scans revealed a large tumor lying on the pancreas, and it was already intertwined with the major blood vessels. The surgeon's blunt words to

Adam were, "You have pancreatic cancer and there is nothing we can do. You have only two-and-a-half months to live. I'm sorry."

We had to deal with this—but how? Adam and I knew we would be walking into the unknown and we decided to walk it together—with Jesus.

Adam had always loved the character of Jesus; in fact, when he was only 12 years old, he came home with a print of Him. I can still see him standing in the entrance of our home under the crystal chandelier, looking at me and asking, "Mother, may I please hang this picture in my room?" I was astonished! I looked at him and then at the picture he was holding in his hands. It was Jesus in full color. We were a Jewish family and had always followed Jewish traditions. We believed that Jesus was merely an ancient teacher, certainly not the Messiah, and His picture had no place in our home. It was unthinkable. Yet, for some unknown reason I remained calm, my voice stayed steady, and I answered softly and thoughtfully, "Certainly, Adam, you can hang the picture in your bedroom." I was amazed at my response until many years later when I became a believer in Jesus as my Lord and Savior.

Adam had gone on to study religion at a leading university, but he still did not receive Jesus as his Lord. During that time, however, I came to know Jesus Christ as the lover of my soul, and three years later Adam accepted Him. He became a beautiful and faithful believer and his love for Jesus was deep. All the study and groundwork that had been laid in his life paid off—his search was over! He thrived under the tutelage of the Holy Spirit and lived a strong, vibrant Christian life for six years before he became ill.

I told you the foregoing in order to prepare you for how we dealt with the sad prognosis that Adam received from his doctor. Adam and I knew the Lord would walk alongside us as we went on this journey, and we talked a lot about it. I must admit, however, that at first Adam was in denial. He accepted an invitation to accompany his best friend to Europe, all expenses paid. He applied for his passport, and made all kinds of arrangements for the trip. This was one of the most difficult phases for me to go through, because he was so hopeful. Needless to say, he never made that trip.

I prayed fervently that Adam would be healed by the power of God. I had already lost my beloved mother and my dear husband to this identical disease, and facing another loss seemed too crushing to consider. I knew God could work miracles—but I also knew I had to wait on Him and be prepared for the worst.

Before long, circumstances caused Adam to accept the truth of his condition and he did so brilliantly. Why do I say that? Well, because it seemed like the Lord lived in my home, where I had brought Adam after his diagnosis. It became a place of worship and peace. It was incredible! Adam called every friend he ever had—Jewish and non-Jewish, believers and non-believers. He had set his mind on only one thing: everyone was to hear and accept Jesus as Lord! He had two-and-a-half months, just as the surgeon had predicted.

At least twenty-five people received a strong witness during this time of waiting for the Lord to take Adam home. He called men he had not seen since his early school years and they either went out for dinner or visited at our home. Adam told each one about the glory of Jesus—and he showed them the picture of Jesus he had brought home so many years before. Now beautifully framed, it hung on the wall at Adam's bedside. He still had it after all those years!

What did Adam and I do together to cope with this terminal illness? Would you believe it if I told you we talked, laughed, and turned on the radio and danced on the kitchen floor? We prayed and played worship music on the piano and sang. And, of course, we cried. We felt extremely close during this time. Our home became wondrous because it felt like angels were in it. And, amazingly, we had the "peace that passes all understanding."

At times when Adam told me his body hurt, he also said he could feel God healing him from the inside. I told him that I felt God was preparing him for a new body, a body full of glory.

There were times near the end when Adam became co-matose. I sat and stood for as long as seven hours, singing songs of his earlier days, songs he loved to hear me sing. My voice grew hoarse, but somehow with the Holy Spirit in me, I sounded young and the tone was sweet. I knew when this happened that the Lord was there by my side.

Sometimes Adam stirred and awakened from his coma, and I asked, "Adam, did you hear me sing, read Psalms and pray for you?" He assured me, "Oh, yes, Mother, I heard it all."

Here was my son, sweet and accepting of all he was going through, preaching Jesus to his friends, suffering without complaint, and understanding very well that he was going to heaven soon. And here I was, my heart weeping inside in sorrow at the thought of losing my only son.

How does one do this? It is solely by the *grace of God!* It can't be anything else. After Adam left this world to enter life in eternity, I mourned, of course. I was a grieving mom and at first I had lots of questions about heaven. I took my questions to the Lord and one night I had a beautiful vision of Adam. The Lord showed him to me so I could be at peace and I will never forget how glorious it was. Although I was asleep, everything was very clear. Let me describe it to you:

I saw Adam's shining face—only his face, arm, and hand could be seen. The view of his head was magnificent. It was an absolutely spectacular and brilliant sight. His face was radiant and his smile was dazzling; his teeth could best be described as perfect caps of white pearl. His entire face seemed to be etched in a glow that is beyond description.

With my eyes I beheld the splendor and luster—shades and hues of pale golds, soft pinks, and colors of ivory and gold running through his glorious face. It is almost too wonderful a vision to describe; he had such an exquisite look. Adam was literally sparkling!

I believe this vision was given to me, a loving mother, as a gift from the Lord so that I would always know what Adam looks like in his new abode, which, indeed, is heaven.

I haven't spoken a lot about the tragedy of losing a son, of how much it hurt. I suffered while I watched my son suffer, but the message I want to convey is that it is possible to come out of the wilderness of that experience with joy. Despite what it feels like or looks like, I actually had the joy of the Lord through it all. It is inexplicable how I, a mother, could lose a child and still feel so tightly woven into the Lord God, who sustained and satisfied my heart.

## How Can Somebody Just Be Dead?

In 1998, an oil well tank exploded while the workers were capping the well just south of Shreveport, Louisiana. Six men were killed that day—and one of them was my brother, Ken. For four days the oil burned out of control and no bodies could be recovered until the fire was out.

When I told my mother what had happened, she suffered a heart attack and had to be hospitalized. When my dad heard, he tearfully asked, "Can you believe it?" No, I couldn't believe it! My life went into slow motion!

My only sister heard the news in another state where she lived, and had to make the emotional, sad flight home by herself. Such sorrow filled our hearts. Suddenly the pain suffered by the families of the Oklahoma City bombing victims became personal and very real to me. I had *seen* their pain, but now I *felt* that same pain. I remember thinking, "Everything has changed—in just one day."

My mother remained hospitalized and I would lie on the bed beside her hour after hour, day after day. She would turn on the television at news time and watch the fires still roaring out of control. As the names of the six workers crawled across the bottom of the screen, my mother would cry the saddest cry I had ever heard. I wanted to run—and just keep on running! If only I could close my ears so that I wouldn't hear my mother's crying. How desperately I wanted to put things back to the way they were before this terrible accident occurred. Sleep was far from me at night and I pictured myself putting my head in the lap of Jesus. I asked Him to hold me so I could drift off to sleep—and He did.

For days, pictures of the fire made the headlines. We waited and hoped. Maybe somehow the men got away—but deep down, I think the Lord was preparing us for the worst. Our hearts were truly broken and tears came from nowhere, it seemed. I honestly wondered if we would ever again have a "normal" day. How I longed for an average, uneventful day; I needed a routine so that my mind could settle down and my insides could be still.

"How can somebody just be dead?" I asked myself this question one day while driving home from the hospital. "How can our family unit be undone? Why did Mom and Dad have to lose a child at their age? How can I not have a brother to call? How can he not be here each Christmas to give me my box of chocolate-covered cherries (a family tradition between the two of us since childhood)?"

It seemed so unreal; after all, I had just talked to him a few days earlier when we had run into each other at the grocery store. *Sometimes I still go to the store and stand in that aisle, right where we were, and just cherish that last conversation.*

My brother was supposed to leave work at noon on the day of the explosion, which happened at 2 o'clock in the afternoon, but he had stayed to help others. He had taken the place of another young man in "the bucket" and as that young man walked to his truck, he heard the explosion. Several other workers in the area were badly burned, but this young man had no injuries. *No greater love—there is no greater love.*

My mother was not able to attend the services for Ken. The news media filmed the services and it seemed like a really bad dream, even when you watched it on the news.

Shock is a strange fellow and the normal functions of the body seem to put you on "autopilot." I believe the Holy Spirit steps in at that time and gives you strength for the moment. I know for me, He was there in every instance—even when heart-wrenching cries welled up within me and I felt almost out of control. *He is in control!* The motions of life may make me feel like I'm in a fog, but I know He is the lighthouse in the middle of that fog.

God knows our every need; He knows the void we now have in our lives; He knows the heart of a father and mother. He allows the sun to come up and the stars to shine—and in the depth of the night, He allows me to lay my head in His lap and sleep.

He allows us to draw on a well of memories; He gave us the privilege of having this special person in our lives. Even though the pain of losing him is so severe, I would still take the pain rather than never having known this wonderful brother of mine.

My Sunday school teacher asked me to explain to the class how we made it through this storm. My answer is still the same: Jesus Christ must be your focus—at all times—in all situations.

## "God, What Do You Want?"

In early 1999, I had just quit a job I had held for ten years as a construction equipment operator to start my own small construction business. My wife was home schooling our six children and my goal was to become self-employed so the children could work beside me and learn a good work ethic. The goal was to use the construction business as a missionary tool for the whole family.

In March of that year, Karen, my best friend, my wife, and the mother of my children died while giving birth to our seventh child. We were living for God and doing all the "right" things, and while I knew that didn't guarantee us a pain-free life, I thought we would be able to bear our trials *together.*

One night a year or so before she died, my wife came to me crying. God had just shown her that we should lift our children up to Him with "open palms" as an act of worship. God used an illustration by Corrie ten Boom in *The Hiding Place* to show Karen how to "let go." My wife had a peace about this, but it terrified me. She kept encouraging me to trust God in all areas of our life, children included, but I couldn't do it—not yet, anyway.

When we found out Karen was pregnant again, we started preparing for the new child. The baby was in trouble from the start and Karen lost a lot of blood during the entire pregnancy. We believe that God is the author of life and all life is precious, so we did all we could to give this child every possible chance to survive.

During an emergency C-section during the fifth month of her pregnancy, Karen received over 30 units of blood; then she was put on a ventilator and given morphine for pain. As the night wore on, she waged a desperate fight for life. She could not talk, but she would look at me and we devised a method of communicating by squeezing hands, blinking eyes, and going through the alphabet to spell out words. I was able to tell her that our new baby was alive and that I loved her.

I cried out, "God, what do You want? I know You can heal her; why don't You?" I sat by Karen's bed and read from the Bible. I had absolutely no doubts about God's healing power in the name of Jesus. I knew that Karen could have stood and walked out of that hospital room at anytime. Yet, God was not healing her (physically, anyway). He was preparing me. I learned that night what she had learned a year before: I needed to open my hands, lift them up and praise God, and trust Him in all things. In the middle of my darkest night, God began to speak. *I wanted a miracle and He wanted to discuss His nature.*

Many hours later, sitting beside her bed, by the power of the Holy Spirit I was able to lift up my hands and give my wife, our new baby, the rest of our children, and my life completely to Him. That's when He revealed His nature to me and gave me the grace to see Him as He is.

"Do you believe I am a loving God?" the Holy Spirit asked.

"Yes," I replied. "You are a loving God and no matter what happens here tonight, I will not question Your nature."

My wife died and I still had questions. "What about our plans, God? Who will teach the children? Who can guide them and love them like their mother?"

Gently He began to instruct me: "You do not need to know *why* at this time; you need to know *how* to trust."

We had no insurance and no money, and the old farmhouse we were renting was going to be sold soon. I was determined to continue home schooling the children, but how could I be father, provider, teacher, mother—and still pay large medical bills?

I didn't know how I was going to do it, but after Karen died, I walked out of the hospital with one unshakable truth: God is a loving Father and He provides for His own. Sixteen days after Karen died, our new baby girl went to heaven, also.

God worked many miracles for us during the next year as His people pitched in and poured out love upon our family.

Hundreds of people helped me turn an old farmhouse into a home. He also provided a young woman to help with cleaning, cooking, and doing mountains of laundry. Best of all, she loved and listened to the children, becoming a rock for them to lean on during those first hectic months. They still get excited when they receive a card or letter from her.

I was often tormented with the memory of Karen fighting for her life. I tried to remember her with the light of life in her eyes, but all I could see was death. I could feel myself falling into depression when one night suddenly before me was a vision of Karen, so perfectly alive in Christ, shining and healthy. No pain, just pure joy on her face.

"See her as she is now," the Holy Spirit seemed to say. "She is alive!" Someday we will all be together with Jesus— me, Karen, and our seven children.

God is good! Armed with that knowledge, I have no fear for today or for the future. God will always be enough—for any situation.

## Heart Attacks, Strokes — What's Next?

My husband, Gene, suffered his second heart attack in 1997, but since the pain was not as severe as he had experienced during his first attack, he ignored the symptoms. Because of his delay in getting medical attention, he sustained significant damage to his heart.

Several months later, he developed a severe case of pneumonia, as well as blood clots in both lungs. This condition lasted for six weeks, and he was in the Intensive Care Unit thirty days in critical condition. He was on a respirator and his condition worsened daily. I began to make preparations for his death but something one of the doctors said made me change my mind. On a Sunday morning, Gene's physician, Dr. Moore, asked me if my husband had a living will and I replied, "Yes, but it's at home." Dr. Moore told me I'd better go home and get it, and for some reason that made me extremely angry. I told him we hadn't come to the hospital for my husband to die, but to get well.

"Your husband has been on two different antibiotics for three weeks and he hasn't improved."

"Well, if those two antibiotics aren't working, then maybe you'd better try something else," I replied. Even though my husband was at death's door, during my confrontation with his doctor, faith and anger at the situation like I had never known rose up in me. In my spirit, I cried, "NO! This is not right!"

That very day marked a turning point in Gene's condition. Within a week he was out of the ICU and he came home shortly after that. In December he was able to have surgery to replace a leaky valve in his heart chamber, and we had a wonderful Christmas.

In January and February of the next year, my husband suffered five or six strokes. None of them permanently paralyzed him, but he was mentally impaired and his sense of direction was affected. This meant I had to drive him to work a few hours a day after his strength built back up. The remainder of 1998 was uneventful, but we both knew he was in danger of "the big stroke," so we spent every minute together. We had many heart-to-heart conversations to make up for the talks we'd let slip by over the years.

In late January, 1999, I came home from church one Sunday morning to find Gene resting on the sofa watching television. He looked up and surprised me by saying, "Honey, can you ever forgive me for the way I treated you all these years?" I quickly thought to myself, "I went to church and while I was there, the Lord and my husband were going over some things here."

"Yes, you already are forgiven. All that is in the past. We're going to press forward now." In my heart it felt like the last piece of the puzzle had been put in place and I had a feeling of great peace and assurance that everything was right. I thanked God for His mercy in giving us that extra time so that everything would be settled between us.

On March 1, 1999, as we were getting ready to leave for a doctor's appointment, Gene suddenly lost his balance and began to fall. I was near him when it happened, so I was able to push and "guide" him over to the sofa. This was "the big stroke" we had feared. In just seven days he experienced another big stroke, which did a lot of damage. He had no short-term memory and no reasoning skills, and he was unable to communicate. He didn't even recognize family members or close friends. How painful this was for everyone!

Our doctor told me to find a nursing home where he could receive 24-hour care. I found an Alzheimer's facility within a mile of our home, so I was able to see him twice a day, every day. At lunchtime and dinnertime I would go to the facility and feed him. I would also bring all his dirty laundry home and wash and press it. This routine went on for nineteen months.

During this time, about six months before my husband died, it was discovered that I had an aneurysm in my head. I was told that if I wanted to live, I had to have surgery right away. Otherwise, it would burst and kill me instantly. Of course, I had the surgery and had to stay in the hospital ten days. After one week at home for recovery, however, I resumed my usual routine of going twice a day to feed my husband, plus doing his laundry.

It is difficult to describe how totally alone I felt during this long, drawn-out sickness. It was such a comfort to know that the Lord was with me, even though I didn't always feel His presence. I just rested in the assurance that His Word said He would never leave me—and that settled the matter.

For several months before Gene died, I felt that the Lord wanted me to speak at his funeral. God had shown me many living examples of His character and His truth through the daily contact with Alzheimer's patients. I knew I had a message in my heart that God wanted me to share, so I did. God empowered me to walk up to the platform and speak the things He had given me. I spoke of God's faithfulness and the uncertainties of life, then I told the people that the most important decision we will ever make is choosing where we spend eternity. Our pastor then gave an invitation and four people raised their hands for salvation. Praise God!

A major lesson I learned through our ordeal is this: Whatever happens in life that you feel is too horrible to bear or is the worst thing you can imagine, God will always be there with you. You cannot escape His presence. And when you are in the midst of severe trials and adverse circumstances, God becomes more real and more personal than ever before. When we are totally helpless and hopeless in any situation, God is there!

## How Will I Know Daddy?

Jessica met Glenn on a blind date set up by a mutual friend from church. After an initial reticence and reserve, the two found that they could talk for hours and their sharing began to grow into love.

"Glenn wanted two things in life," says Jessica. "A happy marriage and children." Both those dreams came true for Glenn when he and Jessica were married and had a beautiful little girl, Shelley.

When Jessica was pregnant with their second child, the fabric of their lives began to unravel. The couple was on a short trip when Glenn started feeling bad. He thought he had the flu, but went to the hospital as a precaution. Doctors also thought flu was likely, but decided to keep him overnight for some tests. Thinking everything was fine, Jessica went home to get some sleep.

About an hour later Jessica received a phone call from the doctor that left her in disbelief. "Glenn needs a new heart," the doctor said. A new heart? Glenn had shared with her that he had some heart problems, but this was more than Jessica could digest. She found out that his heart was double in size and only 14 percent of it was functioning. He needed a transplant immediately!

Glenn was transported by ambulance to a hospital in a nearby major city where his condition could be properly treated, and Jessica followed in her own car with family members. She recalls it as the loneliest drive of her life.

Jessica was a nurse and she requested and received a leave of absence from the hospital where she worked. Her fellow employees donated hours and hours of vacation and sick days to her so that she could stay near Glenn.

In about a month, the doctors felt Glenn was stable enough to go home where he could wait for an available heart. Jessica remembers that they lived life just waiting for the beeper to go off. In fact, she was so obsessive about him that even when he was in the shower, she would knock every two minutes to be sure he was okay. Finally, Glenn said, "Look, Jessie, we can't live like this. We have to get back into a routine and we have to trust God." He was right.

Jessica went back to work and Glenn stayed home and took care of their daughter. They settled back into a fairly normal schedule, laughing, talking, and working through little things just like any other couple.

Then, one evening in August, Jessica's husband, best friend and living miracle paused in mid-sentence at the dinner table. At first those at the table thought he was "goofing around" but he wasn't. Instead of his brilliant smile, his face was frozen in a grimace and his eyes were rolling back in his head. Glenn was having a heart attack!

Jessica had always thought she would panic if this happened, but she was calm and efficient. As Glenn had told her, "God will give you peace, strength, and control if you will trust Him." Jessica quietly gave instructions to those at the table—take Shelley into the other room, go get the neighbors, hand me the phone, I have to call 911—as she watched death take over the man she loved. It was 6:10 P.M.

At 7:15 P.M., despite the efforts of neighbors, paramedics and doctors at the hospital, Glenn was pronounced dead and Jessica became a widow. In her own words, she says, "I was crying, but as I sat there watching people work on Glenn, my whole being was flooded with strength and peace. It was God letting me know in my heart that it was time for Glenn to go." There is a certainty about her faith that she says she got from Glenn.

When she returned home from the hospital and went into Shelley's room, the calmness evaporated. Shelley looked so tiny, so vulnerable, that Jessica cried out to God, "Who's going to take care of us now? How will I tell her that she'll never see her daddy again?" Then the unborn baby kicked and Jessica dropped to her knees beside the bed and wept, "Who will take care of this baby? What does our future hold now that everything I have lived for is gone?"

Then Jessica looked up and saw a Scripture that she had memorized years ago: "For I know the plans I have for you, declares the Lord, plans to prosper you and not to harm you, plans to give you a hope and a future." (Jeremiah 29:11)

Jessica didn't think she was strong enough to make it on her own as a single parent, and lots of people agreed with her. But she *has* made it! A couple of months after Glenn's death, her second daughter, Noelle, was born—one day after Glenn's birthday. Jessica has been able to keep the small home the family has always lived in and she testifies that their lives are full of little miracles.

Jessica made the choice to be happy and content rather than defeated and miserable. She knows that Glenn would want her to really live and now, over five years since his passing, she is doing just that.

Jessica shares, "Faith is evidenced in things not seen, but believed. Glenn had that kind of faith and I got to live with that. He treated every day as if it were his last on earth. I was raised Christian and I believed and trusted God, but it wasn't until my time with Glenn that I realized I was only giving God 90 percent and keeping control of the other 10 percent. Once I truly let go and gave God 100 percent, I found that it doesn't matter what comes my way. Everything first has to pass through His hand and He will provide."

Shelley has vivid memories of her daddy who, as she says, was taken to "live in heaven with God when I was not quite two years old." In fact, she has her very own special way of communicating with her father. She sends him presents every chance she gets. Unlike most children, who tie a helium balloon to their wrist immediately upon receiving it so it doesn't float away, Shelley always lets hers go. She stands and watches it float up until she can't see it anymore then, as she tells her mom, she knows "Daddy has it in heaven."

Shelley's little sister knows that Daddy went to live in heaven before she was born and sometimes this troubles her, but words from big sister have eased her worries.

Recently Noelle asked, "Shelley, when I get to heaven, how will I know Daddy?"

Shelley simply answered, "Just look for the man holding all the balloons. That's our daddy!"

## I Was Never Out of His Sight

On a warm evening in May, I boarded a plane in Oakland,

California, bound for New Orleans to be reunited with my husband, Joe, after a three-week separation. Very tired from taking care of my mother after her recent breast cancer surgery, I looked forward to being with my husband of 35 years.

Joe was a truck driver and we spoke by phone almost every evening when he was on the road. He had called the night before and said his company had scheduled him for an additional stop in Texas on this trip, so he probably wouldn't make it home to New Orleans until the day after I got there. That also meant we would be out of touch by phone for the night I was flying. Some of his last words to me were, "Honey, can't you go one night without talking to me?" They were gently spoken words, yet neither of us had any idea how long that "night" would be.

My plane had a layover in Dallas and most of the passengers disembarked. As we gathered back at our gate and prepared to reboard, I noticed four police officers, accompanied by two airline personnel, approach the counter. My first thought was, "They must be looking for somebody *really bad.*" Then one of them called out my name. My mind flew to my mother; I had been reluctant to leave her so soon. But, no, it wasn't Mom, it was Joe. They told me he had been in an accident and I should come with them.

My mind tried to figure everything out at once. Why did it take four policemen to tell me that Joe had been in an accident? I was suddenly overwhelmed with the awareness of the Holy Spirit's covering—that's when I knew it was serious. I have had lots of practice over the years discerning His presence.

The officers told me to come with them and in the privacy of an anteroom, they told me Joe had been killed. Here I was, all alone in Dallas, facing the staggering news that my husband was gone. What was I to do? In answer to my silent cry, some remarkable things started to occur.

The Holy Spirit led me to recall that Joe's sister, Ella, and her husband, Ted, were to be in Houston in a couple of days for a graduation, which meant they wouldn't be too far from where I was. I was told that there was debate about whether to take Joe's body to Houston or Dallas. "Make it Houston," I said. One of the officers helped me locate Ella and Ted's host in Houston and we got him on the telephone.

"Hey, Ella and Ted just got here about ten minutes ago." Ted said he had felt a great sense of urgency to drive long days and arrive a day early. I could only thank God for His provision for me. Ella and Ted had "parented" Joe from the time his mother died when he was 14, so they were exceptionally close.

The airlines had one more plane leaving for Houston that evening, but the flight was full. However, they were able to find someone who volunteered to give up a seat for me. This was but one of many details through which God showed His love and care for me in the next few days.

I need to point out that through the years, God had allowed me to learn to trust Him through many trials and tests. I had uterine cancer, was run over by a car, experienced His miracle of protection in another near-fatal car accident, lost a kidney, and had to file bankruptcy. I considered it training—training to trust Him in all things!

At almost the same time I boarded the plane in Oakland, Joe was involved in a fiery head-on crash just four miles from his destination. We both became airborne—his was just a more spectacular trip! A lone piece of paper flew out of that 70-mile-per-hour crash—a work order from Joe's company. There were no witnesses to the crash, yet one of the first people on the scene was a state trooper. He picked up the paper, saw the name of the business on it, and recognized it as the place where his wife worked. He gave them a call and asked if they were expecting a delivery. "Yes," he was told. "Joe is on his way in."

The chain of events fell together so seamlessly that it was obvious even the most minute detail was ordered by the Holy Spirit. Joe's boss was able to get hold of our daughter in Southern California, who had no idea what my schedule was. However, she gave him my mother's phone number. "Maybe she will know something," my daughter told him. Here's where the puzzle gets very intricate: My sister-in-law, Sheila, had taken me to the airport and dropped me off at the terminal. Instead of going directly back to her home, Sheila went out of her way to drop by my mother's house "just to check in" on her. Sheila was the *only one* who knew my flight schedule, because it had changed several times. And she was at the right place when "the call" came. Only God could have arranged that!

Here I was, a 55-year-old widow, with no income, too young for social security, and not really physically able to hold a full-time job. Most of our savings had gone for my medical problems, and we had only one small insurance policy that might come through. Some questions about workmen's compensation came up and there were doubts about that for various reasons. One of the biggest arguments was location: Joe's company's main location was in Oregon, we lived in Florida, and the accident took place in Texas. Other states paid benefits for only 18 months to three years—but in Texas, the benefits were for life! Of all the states Joe could have been in when he had his accident, God's provision was to take him home from Texas!

Joe and I were at a place of great joy and contentment in our lives. We had a happy marriage and were looking forward to growing old together and being an example to younger couples. We were settled in a loving church and had many friends—then life changed forever. It is so wonderful to know that God doesn't get surprised, though. I was never out of His sight.

Because of my limited income, I cannot afford to live in California closer to my family. Although I am away from them, He gives me much-needed strength as I go to the Word daily: "But they that wait upon the Lord shall renew their strength; they shall mount up with wings as eagles; they shall run, and not be weary; and they shall walk, and not faint." (Isaiah 40:31)

Joe and I were such a team and my first Christmas without him was hard. I was led to think of his first Christmas in heaven—singing with the angels and the Lord. How happy he must be, knowing that he spent his life well.

## Following Abe's Example

My wife, Joyce, and I lived in the Dallas/Ft. Worth area during the 1980's when the economy slid into depression. My partner and I had built up a very successful construction business and when I sold my share of the company to him, I went full-time into real estate development. I had other business interests, as well, and we were enjoying the fruits of success.

I was at my office when "the call" from my wife came: "Roger, hurry over to Rick and Jamie's house. Rick's dead!" Without stopping to say a word to anyone, I rushed out the back door to my car and tore over to see my sister-in-law. What on earth could have happened? My mind raced as I frantically tried to piece together the recent past in order to understand what God was doing.

God had just helped my business associate and me refinance some notes, and we were jubilant in the way He had worked on our behalf. I knew Rick had just had the flu, but I thought he was recovering well. After all, he was only 30 years old and in excellent health. It came out later that he had been misdiagnosed at the emergency room; instead of the flu, he had bacterial meningitis. He had collapsed on the bedroom floor, where Jamie found him.

Our entire family was shocked beyond words, and shockwaves went through the community, as well. Rick had been a rock to all his friends because of his strength in the Lord. He had been going with me to men's Bible study and was growing in his spiritual walk.

Even before this tragedy struck our family, I had been experiencing stress and health problems. After Rick's funeral, my vision of God's leading got very cloudy and I began to go downhill, both physically and emotionally. My income dropped from a healthy six figures to zero almost overnight and I was forced to declare bankruptcy. We lived on our assets until they dried up, and all the stress took a toll on me. I was exhausted all the time and none of the professionals I went to could give me a diagnosis. It wasn't until years later that I was diagnosed with the Epstein-Barr virus, now more commonly known as chronic fatigue syndrome. After my diagnosis, my mom said, "Roger, I'm sure glad to find out there *really is* something wrong with you." Sometimes I thought I might be losing my mind, and obviously others were thinking the same thing.

As things went from bad to worse, I increased my reading and prayer time. I was reading something every moment of the day. I started in the morning with the Scriptures and followed up with books on the character of God and how to find His will. For ten years I devoured two or three books a week.

During this time I did two significant things: First, I vowed to God that I would quit drinking if He would just get me out of the mess I was in. I didn't really have a drinking problem but it was something I enjoyed and I figured I would bargain with God.

Second, I enrolled in seminary. It's unusual for a successful, 40-year-old businessman to just give it all up and go to seminary. Most of my friends thought I was going through some major midlife crisis and they waited for me to come back to reality—but I didn't. I didn't go back to *their* reality, at least. I really enjoyed my study of the Bible and immersed myself in pursuing more of the Word.

Before too long, we ran out of money, so I had to go back to work. Before my financial problems occurred, I had been a workaholic, but I couldn't put that much time in a job now because of my studies. I found a good, well-paying job that suited my schedule and the Lord blessed me. Joyce and I wanted to do the right thing, so we sold our dream home across from the country club and got rid of a lot of our "valuable" possessions.

It is difficult to express the impact that financial collapse and personal loss have on you. We lost friends (at least we had thought they were friends), we lost social status, and it seemed we lost our purpose and direction in life. We had to totally release our past in order to get to a future with eternal promise. Neither of us knew where we were going, but Abraham's life journey came alive for us. I could just hear Sarah asking Abraham, "Abe, we're moving where? Who told you this? God? Oh, really! Well, when do you think He'll tell you exactly where we're going to end up? And what in the world are we going to do when we get there?"

Another of my brothers died suddenly at the age of 42, but this loss didn't take me down like the first one had. Apparently I had grown quite a bit since Rick's death. Although I dread those sudden emergency phone calls, God has helped me learn how to move on.

Joyce and I moved far from where we had lived the "good life" and are now pastoring and sharing what God has taught us. We are finding that many people have gone through much more suffering than we have, but what we went through was about all we could handle. Our marriage nearly failed and only through Jesus did we survive and actually get stronger. My health has slowly returned and we are healing from our emotional trauma.

I want to share a few important things we learned:

1. There is no situation or circumstance that God cannot change or use for His glory. He can untangle and restructure the most difficult relationships with family, friends, and co-workers. There is no pain that He cannot heal, physically, emotionally, or economically. All He requires is a willing heart.

2. Freedom often brings more pain because of our struggle to let go. We are bound in shackles and imprisoned by our social status (where we live, what we drive, how much we own, the type of work we do). Our past with family and friends can also hinder—and we always have to contend with who we think we are. We see God through our own perceptions, which are flawed. When great changes befall us, we fight to keep what we have. Change may be desirable but many times God's method of effecting that change can be very painful.

3. *God provides for us materially.* The wealthy need to learn this lesson; in fact, *everyone* needs to learn that God is our provider. "And thou say in thine heart, My power and the might of mine hand hath gotten me this wealth. But thou shalt remember the Lord thy God: for it is he that giveth thee power to get wealth..." (Deut. 8:17,18) Most of us grow up thinking that we work, and through our own efforts we make a living. But God is our provider.

## Our God Is Able to Deliver...But if Not...

Triumphs, ecstasies, laughter, heartaches, and tears are

emotions all mothers experience. But the most difficult challenge to our faith is to see our children suffer—and sometimes die.

My precious daughter, Grace, only in her early thirties, was a single parent with three small daughters. As she lay motionless on clean, white sheets waiting to be admitted to the hospital, I leaned across and whispered, "Honey, God is still faithful and His Word is still true." She barely raised one thumb on the sheet, our secret signal. At least she was still conscious.

Grace had worked for 12 years at this hospital. Hundreds of times she had walked the halls with expertly documented paperwork for the doctors and nurses, flashing a warm smile at the patients. Everyone loved her. Then she became one of the patients!

I recalled the day we had sat in the office and heard the oncologist make the terse statement that chilled our hearts, "Grace is terminal."

I had glanced over at Grace's once beautiful face, now distorted because a clump of tumors on her skull caused one side of her head to swell horribly. The tumors triggered seizures, something she had never experienced before. More radiation was scheduled to reduce the swelling.

Sitting there stunned, trying to let it all sink in, I was reminded of the title of a sermon preached by my pastor years earlier, "...But if Not." My mind was flooded with memories of stories I had taught in Sunday school, Missionettes, vacation Bible school, and Bible studies in my home—stories of Job's trials and Abraham's willingness to offer his son Isaac as a sacrifice.

I immediately went to prayer. I wasn't prepared to lose another child. We had already lost a daughter to polio years before, and a son who had been born a few weeks prematurely.

Within a few days, the swelling in Grace's face began to

subside. The predicted blindness and mental retardation had not materialized, and in a few weeks her vision was normal. Her mind remained as sharp as ever during the entire ordeal. Her hair returned, even in the radiated areas, and we celebrated with a $1/4$-inch trim, laughing and crying at the same time.

Grace brought wonderful, sometimes hysterical, joy into our lives—I just couldn't lose her now. It was too much for me to comprehend.

Reminiscing was therapeutic, but my mind was jolted back to the present and to Grace's desperate situation as she lay on the hospital bed, responding to my quiet words of encouragement.

"Isn't this a bit much, God, for me to prove my love for You?" I asked silently.

Grace's cancer had first been removed by breast surgery, then it metastasized to the pelvic area. It traveled up the spine, fractured three ribs, and moved across toward a nerve near the stop of her spine. We were informed that when the disease reached that nerve, Grace would become permanently paralyzed from that area downward.

By the spring, inoperable cancer had invaded Grace's lower jawbone. Our big family, consisting of great-grandma and great-grandpa, uncles, aunts, and cousins, came together bimonthly for prayer. We had long since begun to devour the Word, finding new meaning and comfort through the power of the Holy Spirit to gird us up, to encourage our hearts, and to help reprioritize our lives. Time became more precious with every passing day.

Grace declined further radiation, reasoning that the treatment would be as bad as the problem, and her father and I agreed with her decision. In July, Grace accompanied us to church, and at the close of the morning service, one of her dearest friends and prayer partners approached her. "Grace, I just want to ask you this morning again," she said, "do you *really* love Jesus?"

Alexis later told me that Grace hesitated, then looked her square in the eyes, nodded her head, smiled, and replied, "My precious friend, I believe I love my Jesus more today than I've ever loved Him in my life."

That night I gave Grace her usual back rub, tucked her into bed, and said a short prayer. I whispered, "I love you, Sweetheart," and placed her Bible, which was never far from her, under her pillow.

About three hours later Grace became terribly ill with high fever. We rushed her to the hospital, but more tests and x-rays failed to locate the problem. Exploratory surgery the next day didn't help, either, and she grew steadily worse.

We decided her girls should be brought to the hospital at once. Grace recognized them but was unable to communicate. Missy, Brooke, and Kelsey all had something to say to their mother as they held her hand and gave her kisses.

A couple of days later, Grace peacefully went to be with the Lord.

Did our daughter fear death? No, she knew her future was secure in Jesus. But she was afraid to leave her children, even though there was courage amid the fear. One of the many handwritten notes she left behind reads, "Fear knocked at the door; faith answered, and no one was there."

Motherhood, and now grandmotherhood, is wonderful. Even with its heartaches and tears, there are always triumphs and laughter. If there be a "next potential tragedy," I know I'll again remember the declaration of the three Hebrew children facing the fiery furnace, "Our God whom we serve is able to deliver us...but if not..." (Daniel 3:17,18) My trust, as theirs, will remain steadfast in the true and living God.

## Mom, I *Know* It's for a Purpose

Watching our son, Kevin, struggle with cancer was heartrending. In 1991, when he was in his late teens, Kevin was diagnosed with Hodgkin's lymphoma. After a round of chemotherapy and radiation, he recovered and had six good, healthy years. Then, in his third year at a Christian college, he became ill again and had to drop out.

Specialists struggled for months to find out what was wrong with him, but a diagnosis was hard to pin down because his symptoms didn't fit a pattern. Finally, after a bone marrow biopsy, it was determined that he had myelodysplasia (pre-leukemia), and a bone marrow transplant was needed. Kevin's older brother, Cody, was a perfect match and a willing donor. We all thought we were about to see the end of the disease and we praised God for victory!

Kevin did well for about two weeks and then his body started to reject the donor cells. On Easter Sunday, 2000, he became disoriented, lapsed into a coma, and never regained consciousness.

A little over a year before Kevin's death, I had made some especially meaningful entries in my journal which helped me keep things in perspective after he died. I would like to share a few of those thoughts with you.

*Oh, Lord, I trust in you with all my heart, even when I don't understand what you are doing or why. But, God, it's so hard, especially when I see my son suffering. My heart cries WHY? Why does this have to be? As a mother, my instinct is to protect my child. I would gladly take his pain and suffering if I could...*

*I know your heart must have been breaking when you watched your Son suffer and die. You willingly gave your Son for me. I thank you and praise you for the supreme sacrifice that you made on my behalf.*

*Oh, God, I don't have the kind of courage you had. I don't want to sacrifice my son. I don't want to lose him. But, God, he's not really mine. He belongs to you. If you take him back, then help me to be willing to let him go.*

*I release my son to you, God, so you can work your perfect will in his life or in his death, whichever you choose.*

*We may not always understand the paths we must travel, but we know that you go before us and prepare the way...Help me to look past what I can see with my natural eyes, and see what you want me to see with my spiritual eyes. God, give me strength and courage to face each day, and whatever comes my way, help me just to trust you, love you, and praise you!*

As I wrote those words, I meant them, yet I could not fully comprehend the impact of completely submitting to His will until this past year. My family and I experienced great sorrow after Kevin went to be with Jesus. There are some things in life that we will never understand and I've come to the conclusion that Kevin's death is one of those. I could spend my days trying to analyze his sickness and death, trying to make sense of it all, but it wouldn't work. There are times we have to simply trust God—He knows what is best!

I *choose* to trust God and believe that He did what was best for Kevin and, in the long run, what was best for me, too. Therein lies my comfort. Even Keith knew there was some purpose for all his suffering. One of the last things he said to me was, "Mom, I don't understand any of this and I probably never will, but *I know it's for a purpose.*"

Do I have any idea what that purpose is? No, very honestly, I don't—yet! Only God knows the answer to that, but I do know that Kevin's life touched many people. He not only touched people while he was alive, but his death had a profound effect on many people's lives.

Now that my son is gone, I want to honor him. I believe I can do this by living the rest of my life to the fullest, letting each day be an adventure, as he did. I want to be a blessing to someone and reach out to those who are in need or are hurting. I can identify with those who have suffered, and I want to let love and joy reign in my heart and spill over onto others. I give God glory and I trust Him for strength to make it through each day.

My life will never be the same without Kevin. How could it? But I want to allow God to use this pain, agony and loss to make my life *better!* And when I get to heaven and Kevin meets me at the gate, I want to hear him say, "Mom, I'm proud of you!" Most of all, I want to hear Jesus say, "Well done, good and faithful servant."

What a glorious day it will be when we see Jesus and are reunited with our loved ones who are already there!

## Even in Loss, I Gained

My husband, Charles, and I were searching for truth, and during a "David Wilkerson Youth Crusade" in October of 1976, we stepped to the front of the auditorium together. Our lives were changed forever as we made a commitment to God and became born-again believers. I remember walking to the car after the service knowing we had finally found the truth we had been searching for. A burden had lifted from me as I had been led to the Scripture where Jesus said to the Jews who believed in Him, "If you continue in my word, you are truly my disciples, and you will know the truth and the truth will make you free." (John 8:31,32) Indeed, we were free!

Less than a year later, our first child, Hannah, was born six weeks before her due date. She had a lot of health problems, including a hole in her tiny heart. We were very new believers, but God surrounded us with a group of families in our home church that faithfully nurtured us and held us up. We anointed Hannah with oil and prayed and fasted. She had three surgeries, and shortly after turning six months old, Jesus took her up into His arms. We thanked God for giving her to us. Jesus said, "Let the children come to me, and do not hinder them; for to such belongs the kingdom of heaven." (Matthew 19:14)

On the evening before Hannah died, Charles read these verses from the Bible, "Remember Him before the silver cord is snapped or the golden bowl is broken or the pitcher is broken at the fountain or the wheel broken at the cistern, and the dust returns to the earth as it was and the spirit returns to God who gave it." (Ecclesiastes 12: 6,7) The situation with Hannah was out of our hands and we knew that God does all things according to His good and perfect will.

Many Scripture verses helped us know God's sustaining grace and faithfulness through this time of suffering.

"My grace is sufficient for you, for my power is made perfect in weakness. I will all the more gladly boast of my weaknesses, that the power of Christ may rest upon me. For the sake of Christ, then, I am content with weaknesses, insults, hardships, persecutions, and calamities; when I am weak, then I am strong." (II Corinthians 12: 9,10)

"…you will be sorrowful, but your sorrow will turn into joy." (John 16:20)

These same verses carried us through many other trials in life, and I came to lean on His Word more and more. Although I didn't know it at the time, my personal journey of great trials and tremendous loss had just begun.

In early 1982, our second child, Michael, was born six weeks early, just like his sister had been. On his birthday one year later, he was diagnosed with cerebral palsy. Michael was never able to walk and he uses a wheelchair, but his physical limitations have not kept him from excelling in many areas.

God has given him a real gift for creative writing and he now attends college, majoring in English and history, with an emphasis on writing. Most of all, he is an overcomer who embodies the instruction found in Deuteronomy 31:7: "...be strong and of good courage."

My mother, a gentle lady and a big help to me in caring for my son, died unexpectedly of a massive heart attack in 1994. She was only 65 and it was a great shock to our entire family to lose her so suddenly. Her death brought our family together, however, because my two brothers and I had to begin caring for our father, whose health steadily declined after Mom died.

Our lives again changed in an instant in 1998 when my mother-in-law suffered a blood clot at the age of 67 and went to be with the Lord. This was another unexpected loss and we all felt it deeply.

None of these losses prepared me for the death of my loving husband in 1999. He was only 47 years old and had undergone kidney/pancreas transplant surgery. During his lengthy stay in the hospital, we celebrated our 26th wedding anniversary. His death was devastating to me and I miss him dearly.

A few months before Charles died, a friend asked him to share his favorite verse from God's Word and he chose Romans 12:1,2: "I appeal to you therefore, brethren, by the mercies of God, to present your bodies as a living sacrifice, holy and acceptable to God, which is your spiritual worship. Do not be conformed to this world, but be transformed by the renewal of your mind, and you may prove what is the will of God, what is good and acceptable and perfect."

Charles desired to be God's good and faithful servant, and lived according to Matthew 16:24: "If any man would come after me, let him deny himself and take up his cross and follow me." He kept a journal and I find comfort in reading his personal writings. He reflected on his walk with the

Lord and his desire to be close to Him. And then, "Jesus came and took him."

A little less than a month after Charles died, my father died in his sleep at the age of 78. He didn't seem to be able to gain strength after my mother died. We sure do miss the chef of the family and the delectable dishes he used to serve us.

Yes, I've lost many close family members. They have all gone before me, but I have the assurance of eternal life. God gave His only Son for me and someday we will meet again.

> "In my Father's house are many rooms; if it were not so would I have told you that I go to prepare a place for you? And when I go and prepare a place for you, I will come again and take you to myself, that where I am, you may be also." (John 14:2,3)

My name is engraved on the memorial stone alongside my husband's and I have chosen the following verse for it:

> "The joy of the Lord is my strength." (Nehemiah 8:10)

God has been faithful to me through the years and I am so thankful that Charles and I found peace through Jesus way back in 1976. Because of Jesus, even when I suffered painful losses, my spirit gained intimacy with Him and I was able to endure with peace.

## God Is Truly All — and in All — and Through All

An unexpected heart attack killed my husband of 35 years when he was only 55. God was merciful and did not allow Jack to suffer, and I had the assurance that he went to be with the Lord. This knowledge is comforting, of course, but Jack and I were extremely close and losing him was almost more than I could handle. I screamed in anguish, "No! Please, God, no!" over and over. I felt like I was having open heart surgery with no anesthesia.

I was allowed to be with Jack after he died, and the first thing I said to him was that I wasn't mad at him and I didn't feel sorry for him. Because of Jesus, both things were true. I knew Jesus was with me and would see me through and take care of me in Jack's absence. Also, I knew that Jack was with Jesus and would not miss all the things he had accumulated for our imminent retirement. At the beginning, my "faith" was talking, but I knew God would make it all a reality.

When Jack died, I called my pastor's home and when his wife answered the phone, she assured me she would call the congregation to prayer. I knew she would understand what I was going through because she had lost her first husband to a sudden heart attack. I was numb with grief and unable to pray for myself, but I was conscious of Jesus holding my hand—and I wouldn't let go! During the time when I was unable to pray, I felt the strength of the prayers of my church family.

For weeks I read the Psalms, going over and over the verses that contributed to my healing. Soon I began to realize that God had been preparing me in many ways for Jack's death. Three weeks prior to the day he died, Jack had been away on a hunting trip, and I had used the time to draw close to the Lord. The foremost thing the Lord had impressed on me during that time was peace: "Thou wilt keep him in perfect peace whose mind is stayed on Thee." (Isaiah 26:3) This verse and the strength I had gained from those three weeks of seeking the Lord were instrumental in my healing.

Another way God had prepared me for Jack's death was His provision. In the last year, we had made enough money in our real estate business to retire with no financial problems. We had also taken care of a number of other details in preparation for our retirement—things I could not have done by myself. I thank God for these things that were helpful to me as I ascertained His new plan for my life.

After spending several weeks reading nothing but the Psalms, I began to ask God when I would be healed enough to pray for others. The fact that I could ask the question made me realize I was on the road to recovery. I wanted to minister to others as I had been ministered to.

Before Jack died, I was earnestly trying to commit two hours and forty minutes each day to seeking the Lord—a tithe of my time. And I wasn't even coming close! Afterwards, though, I found that it was a matter of survival to spend *at least* that much time with Him in Bible study, fellowship, and prayer. Even though I was incredibly busy taking care of the business and home by myself, I didn't dare give God less time. And when I could, which was often, I would give Him much more time. Time with the Lord was now my top priority, rather than being on down the line somewhere. My pain was so great and the responsibilities so overwhelming that spending time with God was a matter of life and death. I spent one hour in the morning walking with the Lord after forty minutes of Bible study, then in the evening, I spent another hour walking with Him. During those hours I poured my heart out to the Lord and, in turn, He comforted me, strengthened me, and enabled me to finish all the business Jack had started in our company. I received remarkable grace to do all that I had to do each day. He actually worked miracles in this area.

As soon as I was able, I wrote letters of Christian witness to everyone Jack and I had ever done business with, as well as all our family members, friends, and neighbors. It took me several months to write well over a thousand letters, each proclaiming God's grace and faithfulness to me. I also included an invitation that told them I wanted to be sure that they, too, would be with the Lord when their time comes. I included two pamphlets written by my pastor that clearly explained the gospel and how to be born again.

Caring people gave me books on the subject of handling grief, and I was very grateful for them. They showed me that

God was with me, but I must say that my hours of walking with the Lord, studying His Word, and keeping my mind on Him brought my healing. Some authors advocate God, prayer, and Bible study, but others state the "stages" of grief and outline how you can get through them. I honestly never went through guilt and anger and confusion and some of the other emotions mentioned, and I'm grateful. God healed me in record time and comforted me daily. I realize I have been blessed beyond measure.

I am living proof that God can take your worst nightmare and turn it into your greatest blessing. After I felt well enough to leave the Psalms, I began studying in Proverbs to see how I should conduct the rest of my life. God soon showed me that ministry to Him was the only thing that could possibly make my life worthwhile. It's been a year now since Jack left, and I'm very thankful for God's healing in me. I realize He didn't heal me by applying salve to a wound, medicine to a disease, or binding to a cut, but He healed me with Himself. I stood strong on two verses: "I am the Lord that healeth thee" and "He sent his Word and healed them." Jesus is the Word and truly He has healed me.

My future promises to be even more fulfilling than the life I had with Jack. God can do that! What could possibly be more fulfilling than spending your time, talent, and resources on the Great Commission? I treasure the time I spend with the Lord and I yearn for a deeper relationship with Him. God is truly all, and in all, and through all!

---

## "It Was a Tragic Accident — We Forgive Him"

### THE TRAGEDY

Chris and Lisa Russell were highly respected, long-time residents of a small, picturesque community in Colorado and were bringing up their four children with strong Christian values. The oldest, Brandon, was already out on his own, but their three lively daughters filled their home with laughter and challenge. After all, they were *adolescents!* Megan was a junior in high school, and Cheyenne and Haley were in middle school.

Cheyenne, 14, was a kind, wise eighth-grader who always looked on the bright side, and Haley, 12, was a born leader, bubbly, loving, and helpful. What happened to them on that cold winter morning in 2000 brought grief beyond description. The girls were struck by a car as they darted across the highway in front of their house just minutes before the bus was due to pick them up for school. Cheyenne was killed instantly and Haley was taken to the local hospital, critically wounded. The family, their pastor, and friends immediately gathered at the hospital and began their prayer vigil for Haley. How they were hoping for a miracle!

The hospital waiting room became a scene of wrenching sorrow when the family was told that Haley had died—their second daughter to leave them. Chris, Lisa, and their remaining children nearly crumbled from the pain that engulfed them, and those around could only watch in tearful desperation. Pastor Simmons wept with them and wished with all his heart that he could speak resurrection into the situation—in fact, he even prayed for it. But God answered in His own way.

## GOODBYE

After about half an hour of unspeakable tearing of the soul, the family and Pastor Simmons were invited to go into the room where Haley's body was being held. She was so broken and bruised from the accident and from the medical procedures used to try to save her that she did not look like herself. Pastor Simmons retreated to the background as the family whispered tender goodbyes to the baby of their family. When the Russells were ushered into an adjoining room,

Pastor Simmons went to Haley, touched the cold skin of her bruised face, and whispered his own sad farewell. Then he joined the family.

What happened next deeply touched Pastor Simmons. The devastation and grief in the room was palpable, but Chris began to pray through his anguish. The presence of God moved into the room in a precious, tender way. Then Lisa prayed, followed by the others—and healing began at that moment, although the long, arduous process is ongoing. As soon as everyone had prayed, the nurse came into the room and said the media had picked up on the story and wanted a comment from someone. When Chris asked Pastor Simmons to speak on their behalf, he asked, "What do you want me to say?" Even though he had just lost two daughters, Chris's clear, immediate answer was, "Tell them that it was an accident, a very tragic accident, and we forgive the man who hit the girls."

## AFTERMATH

"Why did the girls run across the highway? The bus usually picks them up just yards from their front door, then turns around and heads back toward the school."

That was one of several questions asked during the time of mind-numbing confusion that lingered after the mishap. Family, friends, and police officers were left with few answers. It was almost like everyone tried to deflect their suffering by concentrating on details of the accident.

The entire area was shaken by the death of the sisters, of course. To add to the shock, the driver of the car that hit them was Officer Dan Parker, a member of the local police department. One of his primary duties was to work closely with school officials and the students, teaching them to avoid drugs and alcohol. Cheyenne and Haley were popular at school, and the fact that the well-liked Officer Dan had caused their deaths added grief upon grief for their classmates. The family had extended forgiveness to Office Dan and even had him speak at the funeral, which undoubtedly helped the students cope.

## GOD'S GRACE

The Russell family was held together by the love of friends and family, and the grace of God. Pastor Simmons supported them on a personal, spiritual level, and took a strong role in dealing with the media. The community at large came together in a remarkable way to meet their needs, both physical and emotional. Everything that could possibly be done for a family in a time of such crisis was done; some would say that this care was exceptional. Yet, real struggles began after the funeral. Grief is a solitary journey and members of the family had to learn to find their way individually and as a unit.

## GUILT

Lisa's battle with guilt started right away: "If only I'd been like those good moms who get up in the morning and make breakfast for their kids, this wouldn't have happened." Even though her mind told her there wasn't anything she could have done if she'd been up, she seemed to feel a need to blame herself. Both girls had been unplanned pregnancies and she found herself thinking, "If we had wanted them more at the beginning, God wouldn't have taken them back." Upon closer examination, Lisa realized that these thoughts came from deep-seated memories of her own upbringing. Her father had a habit of taking a gift away from her if she didn't show enough appreciation, and she thought maybe God was treating her the same way. "We must not have cherished Cheyenne and Haley enough, so God came and took them back." At other times she felt that she must have been a really bad mom, and God had reached down and "rescued" the children.

Lisa discussed her feelings with friends who told her,

"Lisa, you know that's not true." "You're sure?" "Yes, it's not true, it's not true." She soon learned to combat irrational thoughts by just speaking to herself, "You have to take that thought captive; it's not real, you know that." And within a month or two the truth slowly sank in—the scriptural truth that her daughters had a set number of days on earth allotted to them. "Your eyes saw my unformed substance, and in Your book all the days [of my life] were written before ever they took shape, when as yet there was none of them." (Psalm 139:16)

## THE ROCKY ROAD TO HEALING

Chris felt no guilt about the girls' deaths. He realized that Lisa was dealing with a lot of "if only" issues, but his conflict took a different turn. His relationship with his daughters had changed dramatically within the last year because God was changing *him.* He had been enjoying an honest, open exchange with them—and he wished with all his heart that this change in him had taken place three or four years earlier so the improved relationship could have been longer. A couple of weeks before the accident, he and Cheyenne had had a conflict and he had lost his temper, but the next day he had apologized. One of the first things he thought when he found out she was gone was, "Oh, thank God, I apologized to Cheyenne. Thank God." Still, he was angry with God because of the lack of time he had to spend with his daughters, and questioned, "Why couldn't I have been doing it right all along?" He was just beginning to be proud of the father he was becoming.

People respond to tragedy in different ways because everyone is unique. Pastor Simmons saw evidence of this when he telephoned the Russell house. If Lisa answered, she would tell him, "I'm doing okay today, but Chris has had a couple of really rotten days." Then another day Pastor would talk to

Chris, who said, "I'm doing all right, but Lisa is having a very tough time." Another day one of the children might be fighting an uphill battle.

## COMMUNICATION

It seemed that talking became the major avenue to healing, but this didn't happen quickly. For instance, Chris would urge Lisa to talk, but she would say to him, "I don't want to talk. It just hurts when we talk, so don't discuss this with me." While Lisa knew that Chris hurt as much as she did, she felt, "I'm empty. I don't have anything to give anybody. Chris must be empty, too, so why would I want to go to him? *I need something*—I need to be lifted up and comforted. At least my friends aren't as devastated as I am." So Lisa went to her friends, who were always there for her. What she came to realize, however, is that not one of *them* actually knew what it was like to lose Cheyenne and Haley—*and Chris did*.

Lisa found that although talking with her friends helped her, ultimately it wasn't as healing as talking with Chris. In fact, Chris, Lisa, Brandon, and Megan all began to talk. They could reminisce about "inside" family events or issues, and savor the memories. They could laugh together about the girls' individual personalities and cry together over something they all missed. Friends wouldn't see the humor in silly recollections nor relate to intimate family matters—just because *they weren't family!*

Grief is like a moving target—it changes by the minute. You may wake up thinking you're going to be okay, but something happens and you fall apart—then you blow your nose and you're okay again. And you can't depend on everyone else in the family being okay the day you're having it rough. It virtually never happens that way. Many times everyone is feeling lousy at the same time and it takes real wisdom to know when to push or when to let it go.

In the beginning, Lisa's crying seemed to upset Megan,

so she told herself, "Okay, that makes her uncomfortable, so I won't cry in front of her. She doesn't want to see me like that." Lisa would try to confine her tears to another room—and then it seemed like Megan did a complete flip-flop. The two of them had a fight one evening and Megan said to her mother, "You just don't feel anything—you're not crying! What's wrong with you? I feel like you're not even human." Lisa responded, "Well, I didn't know the rules had changed." Family members had their own "language of grief," but patience and consideration brought an acceptance of each other. Communication was sometimes uncomfortable and difficult, but understanding each other's feelings helped hasten the process of mending.

### GRIEVING—AND OTHER PEOPLE

There were also misunderstandings with those outside the family. Megan's friends didn't know how to react to her and they looked to adults for guidance. One teacher actually went into her classroom ahead of Megan and told the students *not to make a big deal out of things*. Because of the restraint on the part of the students, Megan mistakenly felt everyone was ignoring her—and it hurt! So you have to be careful when dealing with "this grieving thing."

Lisa saw that people often (usually!) didn't know how to act or what to say. She found herself reacting negatively to people who tried to hug her, because she's not an openly touchy-feely person. She would want to say, "Back off! I need my space." On the other hand, if people didn't approach her, she felt like they didn't care, so it's a double-edged sword. People often don't know how to articulate their concern and sometimes things come out wrong, but you have to give them credit for trying.

Nothing can "fix it" and you have to stumble your way through life a day at a time. Lisa witnessed the discomfort of others many times in the grocery store, for instance. Someone would see her down the aisle and discreetly pretend to have to go the other direction. She knew they didn't mean to hurt her, but she would have felt better if the people had just come up and stumbled over their words, "Uh, uh, uh, I don't know what to say—but I'm sorry."

Lisa and Chris agreed that platitudes don't work when you're trying to deal with a tragic loss. They didn't want to hear, "They're in a better place," or "They're perfect now." Even though it's true, Lisa said, "My brain knew they were right, but I didn't care. I wanted my girls with me, living a crummy life in our house. That's where they're supposed to be." Even quoted Scripture can be irritating at first, because the pain of loss is so raw that you can't really listen. The thing that helped most was hearing the simple words, "This just hurts, doesn't it?" And, indeed, it did!

## SUICIDE

Another thing Lisa grappled with was a temptation to get away from her pain by taking her own life. She could almost hear voices calling her, "Come on! Come on! Your pain will be over. You can do this." She had always lacked tolerance and compassion for people who committed suicide, but now she understood how it feels to want to leave the earth. She thought if she took her own life, the agony would be over and she would be with Cheyenne and Haley. "I'd make sure to say a quick prayer and ask God to forgive me just before my last breath." She thought she was such a mess that her family would be better off without her—the deception of Satan was very persuasive. She had the good sense to talk about her feelings with her friends and Chris, "I'm feeling really dangerous at the moment, so take away the sharp objects." Lisa says she is embarrassed and feels shame about her feelings, yet she knows they had to be brought out into the open. She now walks in a new compassion for people who get so desperate that they even *consider* suicide.

## GOD'S STRONGHOLD

Chris and Lisa both tapped into the reserve of the relationship they had with God *before* the accident, because *afterwards* they had an aversion to reading His Word. Somehow your heart wants to hear personal comfort, not something from the written Word. You are sustained by your foundational relationship with Him, because what you go through after the funeral surprises you. There are questions, so many questions, and anger and confusion. But through it all, God is there, leading you down the right path, helping you work things out. Many times Chris would hear Lisa say, "Yes, I feel angry, *but I simply cannot dismiss what I know to be true.* I'm so mad at God and He's so big and mean, *but I just cannot let go of His truth.*" The *truth* that she had hidden in her heart held her steady in spite of her *feelings* and her words.

## HONESTY WITH GOD

Some may have a problem with such genuine candor with God, but He doesn't disapprove of honesty. He knows how you feel, anyway, so you can't really hide from Him. Grief of the magnitude that Chris and Lisa suffered shakes you to your very core, and Chris began to question his whole belief system of the past twenty years. Was it all just a cleverly fabricated fairytale? Were his girls really just lying dead in the ground? Was believing in heaven and angels and paradise foolhardy?

People would urge Chris to go to the Word for comfort, but it didn't work. He'd open the Bible and read about Jesus raising Lazarus from the grave while his sisters cried. Then he'd scream at God, "Well, haven't we been crying enough? Aren't there enough tears falling around here? We've only gone through a hundred boxes of Kleenex—isn't that sufficient? Why did You raise him and not my girls? Why was he so special? Was it something his family did? Did they give You a special petition and we just don't have the formula?"

So the way Chris was reading the Word didn't comfort him, it just made him mad!

## FUTILE SEARCH

People who have no relationship with the Lord deal with their deep grief in various ways, and Chris and Lisa can understand their desperation. "You hurt so much and you long for comfort. I can understand why people go to séances—I can see where you would go anywhere to realize some sort of peace. You'd use drugs and alcohol, and pay any price for some sort of hope. The pain is so incredible that if you found something to relieve it, you'd do it—right, wrong, or indifferent. I can see where people who don't know the Lord can get real weird very quickly. You're willing to grasp onto anything to give you comfort. Dial your guardian angel? You bet! Just $19.95? Okay, absolutely no problem."

## RECONCILIATION

The good news is that reconciliation came, although it was a slow process. Chris and Lisa had been praying together for a couple of years before the accident and they made a concentrated effort to continue doing this. There were many nights when the prayer was simply, "Oh, God!" Or sometimes it was, "We acknowledge You exist." That was it. Period. They couldn't go beyond that. But they were being honest. Their hearts were shredded and they didn't feel like God was nice or kind or generous or tenderhearted or sovereign. It didn't seem like He knew what He was doing—but they kept trying to reach out to Him. Lisa freely voiced her misgivings. "You didn't consult with me about what You did and I don't think what You let happen to my girls is right!" She felt all the things in her heart needed to come out and she was right, because in the midst of her venting, God gently got her attention, "There, there, it's all right. I *do* have everything under control and I *am* sovereign. *Trust Me.*"

When Chris and Lisa began to come to terms with their feelings, they knew that God was helping them. Chris likens God's intervention to the love and discipline of a real father/ child relationship. There comes a point where you realize that your heart is set on God and He wants to bring you into a more intimate relationship. You no longer want to argue, but your grief and sense of loss are so unsettling, upsetting, ripping, and tearing that you are compelled to discover God in a deeper way. The prerequisite for intimacy is absolute honesty and God saw this couple's honesty. He walked them through their struggle, and in His own way He reconciled them to Himself.

## HEAVEN

Lisa had a pressing need to know about heaven—she wanted to know where Cheyenne and Haley were and what they were doing. She found that the Bible said a lot more about hell than about heaven and that disturbed her. She wanted an outline of what went on, a sequence of events or a timetable. "After you get to heaven, do you check in? Is there orientation? Do you have to go to 'New Saints School' or do you just sit around playing harps? Do you float around?" She couldn't understand why God hadn't been more forthcoming about what heaven is like. She wanted it all written out for her so she would know, "Okay, my daughters are fine. They've been there three weeks and they should be enrolled in 'Cloud Hopping 101' or some such thing." Her lack of knowledge was really disturbing her, and she started mumbling and murmuring, "You're withholding information. You knew I'd want to know this."

God gave Lisa her answer in a beautiful way. Very gently, very kindly, He spoke to her heart, "It's like this…" Then He opened in her mind the whole scenario of a pregnant woman. The world is active and revolving outside the womb and the space between the baby and the outside world is mere inches.

The baby is safe and happy in the womb; it's warm, wet, and dark and that's the only reference the baby has. If the baby could understand, you could explain in eloquent words in every language about what we do out here in the real world, how things look, and how foods taste. You could describe the softness of a kitten, the mouth-watering flavor of chocolate, the beautiful colors of a sunset, and the swiftness of a shooting star, but the baby would never get it. Why? Because before birth, there is no point of reference. You have to be born into this world and start exploring, discovering, and learning. "So you see," God gently said, "it's like that." And Lisa understood that no matter how much research was done or how many volumes were written, no one could ever really fathom what heaven is like. So why should she waste her time wondering anymore? "Oh, thank You, Father."

Lisa still doesn't know a lot about heaven, but she has come to terms with how things are. Now she doesn't question so much, even though she still wishes the Lord would lift the veil just a little bit and let her see what her girls are doing. Any parent can understand that!

## FORGIVENESS

Forgiveness is a sensitive but important issue in a tragedy like the one Chris and Lisa went through. Initially they readily forgave Officer Dan and extended their hand to him through Pastor Simmons, but how did that play out in the long run? Truly there were two distinct sides to this tragedy, and while the family of the girls suffered anguish, Officer Dan and his family undoubtedly endured their own torment. Would it be better to contact Officer Dan or not? Would they feel better if Officer Dan contacted them or just left them alone? Unfortunately, there are no absolutes or well-defined rules to give guidance, because each situation is different—and people are different. Awkward moments can occur without warning and you just muddle through.

Lisa felt like a little more personal attention from Officer

Dan would have helped her, at the same time realizing that his way of coping might be to stay away and "give them their space." One of those "awkward moments" occurred for her when she ran into him at school one day. Ironically, it was close to the day Cheyenne would have turned 15; also, the holidays were coming up and she was feeling pretty blue. She didn't resent just Officer Dan, she resented her friends and everybody who seemed to be going on with a normal life when hers was so shattered. When she saw Officer Dan, she greeted him, and then said, "Look, I'm going to be very rude right now, but I just need to know something. *Have you forgotten?"* Officer Dan's eyes filled with tears as he replied, "No, I haven't forgotten. Every day—it's with me every day." Lisa simply said, "Okay," and the bitterness that had been trying to creep into her spirit was gone. She had admitted that she was having some hurt feelings, she had confronted them, and then she had asked Officer Dan a hard question. Her kind heart let her see that he probably didn't know how to approach the family and he was doing the best he could.

Megan saw Officer Dan at school on a regular basis and sometimes it bothered her to see him interacting with the students. Especially at first, she thought he was acting like nothing had even happened, and she got angry. Then she would feel overwhelming compassion and give him a hug, saying something like, "It's okay, Officer Dan."

Officer Dan and his wife were hurt and they expressed their feelings to others, but it would probably have helped Chris and Lisa if he had been more open with them personally. Who knows what kind of misgivings he was having? On the anniversary of the accident, he may have thought, "I've caused that family so much grief. Are they going to want to hear from me or do they just wish I didn't exist? If I send a card is it going to cause them more grief or will it help? Should I call them or would they prefer not to hear from me?" It's easy to see the two sides of such a difficult situation.

## COMPASSION AND CARING

The Russell family was ministered to long after the funeral. Various churches that they hadn't even attended worked together to help them in many ways. Meals were brought to their home for almost an entire year! One lady organized a "prayer calendar" that covered a year. People put their name and phone number on specific days to pray for the Russell family, then the calendar for each month was given to Chris and Lisa. If they had any special needs, they could call the "designated pray-er" for that day. They will never forget the phenomenal men and women who organized these things, and seeing the names of the people who prayed for them brought such comfort. They could *feel* the effects of the prayer!

## PRAYER

Chris and Lisa want everyone to know how incredibly valuable prayer is. They look at things they are still facing and know that the grace of God is enabling them to "bear the unbearable" because of prayer. They see, feel, and comprehend that their burden is lighter because it is being shared. "Bearing one another's burdens" is a reality in their lives. Walking alongside grieving people requires commitment, because you may have to reach out consistently (and risk being rebuffed at times). "Taking the casserole" is good, but things don't get better right away. As Lisa said, "Grieving people are messy." Gaining this understanding has caused Chris and Lisa to be more compassionate, thoughtful, and patient.

One strong reality that has been driven home to the Russell family is how precious life is, how short time is, and how things can change in one split second. When God takes your loved one(s) and leaves you here, it's for a purpose. When you fully realize there's no guarantee of tomorrow, you try to listen to God and follow His gentle leadings on a daily basis.

# PART SEVEN

# MORE TESTIMONIES
# OF TRIUMPH

## God Delivers Us from Danger Even
## When We Don't Know It

Starting in the fall of 1998, our family went through a series of ordeals that tested our faith. Our first granddaughter, Sarah, was born and we were all so thrilled at God's blessing. At first everything seemed to be all right with her, but it wasn't long before a serious heart defect was detected. The condition, called tetralogy of Fallot, would require open-heart surgery by the time Sarah was six months old. My daughter, Karen, and her husband were understandably distraught and we were all quite shaken. Our family had never had to face such a grave situation before.

Our other daughter, Diane, was pregnant and due to give birth just about the time Sarah was to undergo her surgery. Somehow Diane developed an acute case of poison ivy that got so bad that they put her on steroids to control it. However, instead of improving, the inflammation went into a secondary infection, so they started antibiotics. One doctor remarked that he had never seen such a severe case of poison ivy in all his years of practice. Just when we thought Diane would be getting better, she developed an allergic reaction to one of the antibiotics, so they hospitalized her in order to treat her and observe her progress.

Diane did improve, and just when she was about to be released from the hospital, they discovered that her baby, which was due in a month, was in some sort of distress. The baby's heart rate plummeted and they said that if it didn't improve, labor would be induced, resulting in an early delivery. Sure enough, labor had to be induced, and even as that was going on, Diane was having more problems. Her blood pressure dropped dangerously low but they stabilized her and after many hours, our second granddaughter, Meg, was born. She was so strong that even though she was a month early, she didn't need neonatal care. God had brought us through a major challenge and had delivered my daughter and granddaughter from harm.

Just a few weeks later, we were waiting in another hospital in another city as Sarah faced her surgery. We had been told the surgery would take five hours, then she would have a hospital stay of around ten days. While we waited, we saw many families facing life-or-death situations and we were able to pray and offer encouragement to those going through similar struggles.

Every hour during Sarah's surgery, a nurse would come out and update us on her condition. We found it especially hard to wait when we knew she was on the heart-lung bypass machine. The fifth hour came and went, then the sixth. Finally by the seventh hour, the nurse came out, accompanied by the doctor, and let us know that Sarah was out of surgery. She had tolerated the surgery well and was released from the hospital on the fifth post-operative day. The Lord had brought us through another great trial and we all gave Him praise.

The very next day, I was preparing breakfast and I noticed that our dog couldn't stand up. We were afraid he had suffered a stroke, but we thought he was too young for that, so we decided to watch him carefully. I was still very focused on my granddaughter and told my husband that I wanted to fast and pray for her the next day. When the dog still seemed to be a little "different" the next morning, we took him to the veterinarian for an evaluation. We got to the vet's office before he arrived, so the receptionist had us wait. The waiting room had an area up near the front with a bench for us to sit on. Almost as soon as we sat down, I turned to my husband and blurted out, "Let's go get a quick breakfast!" I had completely forgotten my desire to fast.

My husband gave me a strange look, but agreed, and had the dog put in the kennel in the back of the vet's office. When we sat down to eat at the restaurant, all of a sudden I remembered my commitment to fast. "What am I doing?" I exclaimed. "I'm supposed to be fasting today." My husband told me he had wondered why I had changed my mind, but hadn't said anything.

When we got back to the animal clinic, we understood why God had given me the impulse to leave the office. While we were at breakfast, a car had jumped the curb in front of the clinic and had gone through the front doors into the waiting room. The car landed right where we had been sitting! We could hardly believe our eyes and knew immediately that God had truly delivered us from death in a powerful way, just as He had done in our family in our recent trials. What a time of thanksgiving we had!

Later I found the Scripture that so clearly spoke of all we had gone through the past several months. "Blessed be the Lord, who daily bears our burden, the God who is our salvation. God is to us a God of deliverances; and to God the Lord belongs escape from death." (Psalm 68:19,20) Praise His name. Incidentally, our dog also survived his ordeal.

Through this time of trials, we also experienced several other amazing interventions by God. He has often reminded us of those months when we faced seemingly overwhelming circumstances, and shown us that He was with us in those uncertain times. One trial seemed to build on another until we thought we couldn't endure anymore. I believe He used the episode with the car to demonstrate to us how often He delivers us on a daily basis. He even directs our thoughts and leads us out of danger when we are least expecting it. What an amazing God. We have all grown much stronger in our trust in Him. May His name be praised forever!

## My Husband Is a Sex Addict

I was 33 years old with three young children and a husband who consumed a fifth of gin straight every night, in addition to his lunchtime cocktails and weekend beer. He was a workaholic and spent most nights and weekends out of the house. I had had enough and had chosen a lawyer to get me out! However, Jesus invaded my life in a miraculous and unexpected way and began to reveal His plan for my life.

Two months later, the Lord dramatically and gloriously saved my husband! The next couple of years were like heaven on earth, the marriage I had always dreamed of. But gradually old signs began to reappear: a glass of wine, a couple of beers, a lack of intimacy, the old withdrawal from reality, an angry retort, lies, silence. All these were telltale signs, warning me of danger.

You see, my husband is addicted to sex, abnormal, immoral, perverted sex. In a way, he is harmless, and if you met him, you would most likely enjoy his company—for a time, anyway. As long as conversations are light and superficial, he can be charming and witty.

My husband lives in a fantasy world where he is always captivating, clever, and deserving of everything and anything his imagination desires and creates. He spends more and more time hidden away in his private, perverted place than he does with me.

His sinful life of defeat and guilt has made him angry, selfish, secretive, deceitful, and thoughtless. It has created constant debt and left a path of wounded, bewildered, angry victims. I am one of those victims and I know I am not alone. I know that hundreds, even thousands, of women, Christian and non-Christian, know my pain, anguish, and frustration. I know they relate to my years of confusion and loneliness. I know the smile on the outside muffles the screams on the inside. I know they understand what it means to be what is called an unmarried wife.

During the first months after his conversion, my husband had tempted God and let the spirits back in (worse than before). But now we were both in ministry. Was it safe for me to talk to anyone? Who would believe me? After all, there was no *real* evidence. Maybe I was being too critical, too religious, too old-fashioned.

What I didn't know at first was that God was showing me a very real spiritual fact. Hurtful circumstances, rejections, fears, and confusions of my life before I knew Jesus had caused anger, unforgiveness, bitterness, hatred, and a desire for vengeance. He was letting me see that these feelings were now settling on me again. Only this time, Jesus was in me! This time I could face these circumstances, rejections, fears, and confusion with the Lord Jesus Christ.

I admit I have fallen many times; I had to learn what it means to "be angry and sin not." This was a very slow process for me, but I can assure you of one thing: If you mean business with God and pray from a humble heart (that's a truthful one) for the one offending you (sinning against you), you will eventually end up with God's love for that person, no matter what they have done.

Short of being in jail, there is not much that my husband has not done to hurt me. I can tell you from an honest and hopeful heart that I love my husband and I know God loves him. I've seen God bail him out of one situation after another, and I know that loving him is the prime purpose God still has me on this earth. It is the single hardest thing for me to do and the one area in which I am constantly tempted, but I DO love my husband. If it were not for Jesus, this would be a mystery to me. And if it were not for Jesus, I would not be able to tell you there is HOPE for your battered, bruised, and confused heart.

My husband has a spirit of addiction, and there are many of you women out there who know what I am talking about. You need to ask yourself just how important Jesus is to you. Are you willing to allow the Savior of your soul to melt you, mold you, fill you, and use you? We all want to be used but we shy away from the fire that melts, the circumstances that mold and, all too sadly, the time "in the garden" that fills.

So just stop! Seek the kingdom of God and His righteousness first. Read the Word and be led by the Spirit. Surround yourself with *like-minded* Christians and then remember that this is *spiritual* warfare—and watch out! The walls of Jericho will come tumbling down. Not in an instant, but they will come down.

I want to encourage you to "keep on keeping on." You are called and chosen and you are precious to God, so trust Him. No one else can do for Him on this earth what He has ordained for you to do. He will never leave you!

Burn the "how to" books and read the Word of God! Befriend the Holy Spirit, for He will always lead you to Jesus. Learn that the children of God are led by the Spirit of God rather than by their consciences or peer pressure. The will of the Lord Jesus Christ is that we love one another as He loved us. Love as He loved, for "greater love has no man than this that a man lay down his life (his self) for his friend." Peter tells us the end of our faith is the love of the brethren.

The enemy of our soul sows discord, so we must choose whom we will serve. How important is Jesus to you? The wonderful Holy Spirit will show you that Jesus came to destroy the works of the devil and set free all those who have lived their entire lives in fear (that includes you).

I am a simple woman, a slow learner, but when I look back at the fearful, timid, naïve woman I was twenty-five years ago, even I am in awe at the wonders He has worked in my heart and mind.

- I have HOPE—not that my life's circumstances will ever change, but that Jesus will not change.
- I have JOY—not because my hopes and dreams have come true, but because Jesus has brought me all I could ever think, hope, or dream.
- I have PEACE that passes all understanding because the Prince of Peace lives in my heart and "husbands" me by meeting all of my deepest emotional needs.

I join the apostle Paul in the fact that "I know whom I have believed and am persuaded that He is able to keep that which I've committed unto Him against that day." I know that I can do all things through Christ who strengthens me—and so can you!

I have learned to be patient with myself and not look at what God seems to be allowing others to "get away with." This is my life with God, and His plan for me is special, holy, and perfect. So is His plan for you.

Those of you who walk this same path know what it feels like to be separated yet not separated; to be divorced yet not divorced; to be a one-parent family with two parents. I know you have run away a million times in your heart. I also know you have wanted it to just be over—to end it all. Just as I have! Oh, to simply turn the wheel of the car and hit that tree. It would look like an accident. But my children—who would care for my children? Oh, yes, I know that and so many more of the temptations. Some women have simply ended it with divorce.

I feel I must speak to those who stay. I speak to those who can't quit. I speak to those who fight for their families, those who know with all knowing that this *is* the life that God planned for them. I speak to those who know that this is the life God ordained for them before the foundation of the world—a life of suffering.

Our culture is averse to this thinking, I know, but the Scriptures are not. We read:

- Pick up your cross and follow me.
- Present your bodies a living sacrifice.
- Lose yourself to find yourself.
- Deny yourself daily.

These verses most definitely state with clearness that the way of the cross, what should be normal Christianity, is a way of suffering. Not a morbid or self-pitying suffering, but a joyful giving up of one's self to follow a path clearly marked and directed by the Holy Spirit of the living God.

This is not an easy place to arrive at because self dies hard. Self seeks any possible avenue of escape. In our culture, psychology and women's rights movements have provided wide open doors for that escape. To all who understand this even though their journey through pain may not be the same as mine, I say REJOICE!

What I am sharing with you came neither quickly nor easily, but each step along the way He has been my Comforter, Teacher, Lord, and Giver of Life, the blessed Redeemer, and my Divine Husband who has never left nor forsaken me.

Rather, He has encouraged and admonished me and shed His light on the path—the straight and narrow. It is the way of love. It is the way of mercy. It is the way of forgiveness. It is the way of hope. It is the way of kindness.

Many times I've fallen on this uphill path, but He has helped me up each time with an eager and ready supply of His strength, His grace, and His peace, leaving me refreshed and excited to seek His kingdom first.

## The Prodigal Daughter

In the fall of 1980 while I was in an abortion clinic, the voice of God literally boomed into my dull, heathen brain that I must leave that place right then—with no delay! I was in the armed services at the time and I didn't know how I was going to manage, but I obeyed "the voice." True to His character, God sent one of His faithful servants along to hand me a tract and "get in my face" about my need for Jesus in my life. This "random" encounter resulted in my conversion and I knew He was with me as my beautiful daughter, Josie, was born. Jesus further led my footsteps to meet my husband and we were married about a year later.

Because God literally rescued Josie out of an abortion clinic, I knew He had a marvelous future planned for her. She was a delightful, kind child and everyone loved her. In her teenage years, she was obedient and followed God closely; in fact, many times she fasted and sought God and He spoke to her heart.

After Josie's high school graduation, she planned to marry a young man she had been dating for over a year. Even though she was quite young, we approved of the match and anticipated the wedding. None of us could have foreseen the sudden events that overtook us with lightning speed. Before we knew what was happening, Josie cancelled the wedding, and after an especially stressful day at home, she left. Just like that, she was gone—and the unthinkable happened. She immediately and completely plunged into Satan's kingdom with inexplicable fervor. She cut her hair in a "butch" style and dyed it a dramatic color. She pierced her eyebrow, nose, and tongue, and began drinking and using drugs. She moved in with a wild, partying young man and began dabbling in witchcraft, tarot cards, ouija boards, and other occult "games." Finally Hindu gods and goddesses took over her life, and she was seemingly lost to us.

I was so deeply attached to Josie that I felt like I was going to die; in fact, I mourned for her as for a dead child. For the first three months after she left, my grief was so consuming that I even thought of leaving my husband. Then I mustered the strength to talk to my heavenly Father, "Please! Relieve this heavy sadness and feeling of hopelessness or I might die." Did I *find* the strength or did He *bestow* the strength?

I went through a period of painful introspection, examining our parenting methods and feeling guilty and under condemnation. The Lord told me to *rest in Him* and quit trying to explain everything—to be done with it. He had a divine plan for Josie's life and He would unfold it in time. I felt that His plan encompassed all that had happened and all that would happen.

As Josie moved from place to place, sometimes refusing to communicate with me, God always spoke to me. I filled a journal with His very clear encouragement and instructions. He let me know when she was suffering deeply and gave me wisdom through the Word.

God also gave me promises concerning Josie, such as:

> "Now I will bring Jacob back from captivity and have compassion…they shall know I am the Lord their God which caused them to be led into captivity among the nations…" (Ezekiel 39:25,28)

"Again I will build thee and thou shalt be built, O virgin of Israel: thou shalt again be adorned with thy tabrets, and shalt go forth in the dances of them that make merry...He that scattered Israel will gather him and keep him, as a shepherd doth his flock. For the Lord hath redeemed Jacob, and ransomed him from the hand of him that was stronger than he." (Jeremiah 31:4,10,11)

I was regularly given so many words from God that I was able to rest comfortably by faith, not worrying like I had been. Josie has been in contact with us and she has been hearing from the Holy Spirit again—praise God! She is due to give birth to our first granddaughter soon and we expect her back in our home by the time the baby arrives.

My testimony here doesn't have anything to do with the strength or nobility of *my* personality and character—it has *everything* to do with God reaching down into our desperate situation and filling it with His presence and the Holy Spirit.

God knew we would fall apart as a family if He didn't abide with me and He was so faithful, even when I wasn't. I have learned to trust Him, no matter how bad things look, because *He can be trusted!*

## High Voltage Awakening

Brian knew that God had called him into full-time ministry, which meant he needed more training; in fact, he even knew the seminary that God wanted him to attend. What he didn't know was how he could just drop his 40-hour-a-week job and his pastorate and move his family more than 600 miles to follow his calling.

"I kept making excuses why I couldn't move. I felt there was no way I could ask my family to just pick up and relocate. I'm a hard-headed guy and God had to jolt me a little bit to get my attention." Well, the kind of jolt Brian got was pretty drastic. He was a cable television lineman and knew his job so well he could pretty much do it with little concentration. However, it's never wise to get too relaxed when you're working around high voltage wires.

As he hovered above his cable-laying comrades in an elevated bucket, Brian wasn't really thinking too much about the task at hand. He was more interested in what he was going to have for lunch. Just as he pulled up the last span of cable, intending to tie it off, he grabbed a line that had become entangled with a hot wire.

Without warning, 14,000 volts of electricity—seven times more than the voltage used in an electric chair—surged through Brian's body, blowing holes out his fingers. It traveled through his heart, lungs, and stomach, and then exited out his left side, leaving two fist-sized holes.

Somehow Brian was able to let go of the line before collapsing in the crate. Still conscious, he thought he'd never make it to the ground. His coworkers got to him, lowered him down, and waited for the ambulance, which had to come from a neighboring town. As Brian lay in pain, the only other Christian in his group prayed for him. "That could have a lot to do with why I'm still here today," Brian says.

The doctors in the emergency room and the burn center could hardly sedate Brian as they tried to alleviate the excruciating pain. They wondered if they would be able to salvage his arm. However, their pessimism soon turned to astonishment! Although he had suffered multiple burns both inside and outside, most of his vital organs seemed unharmed. The medical staff marveled. One of the doctors at the burn center told him, "We see high voltage cases occasionally, but most of the guys who get what you got never make it to us."

After five surgeries, numerous skin grafts, and weeks of recuperation, Brian experienced a remarkable recovery. While lying in bed convalescing, he faced the decision he had been putting off. "God, I get the message. No more excuses."

"I knew exactly what I was supposed to do," Brian recalls. "I know most people who have kinda stared death in the face have said this, but it does make you put things into perspective."

Brian checked out of the hospital within two weeks, and six weeks after the accident he was back in his pulpit. He and his family made the move the Lord had directed them to make and today he is studying at a fine seminary.

"God saved my life...He's made it possible for me to study for a reason. I constantly remind myself of that." He readily admits electrocution would not have been his chosen method of correcting his course.

"If God had given me a choice of how I got to where I am now, being electrocuted would not have been on the list," he said, but he admits God's method worked.

"God moved me in the way He wanted me to go," Brian said. "I just give Him the praise and honor and glory for it all because I really shouldn't even be here. From now on, I'll listen a little closer without being so hard-headed about what God has to say."

Brian credits God and the prayers of family, friends, and church for his miraculous recovery.

## Can Jesus Get Us out of This Mess?

"Mom, I'm pregnant!"

The words of my rebellious, fifteen-year-old daughter shocked me out of my alcohol- and drug-induced stupor. Pregnant? How stupid could she be? I had sent Melissa from California to Arkansas to live with my retired parents and I thought she would straighten up her life. It was obvious my "parental guidance" wasn't succeeding. I was in the middle of divorce proceedings and additional emotional stress from my daughter was not welcome.

Melissa had her baby daughter and shortly thereafter I found another husband, Nathan. I sincerely wanted to make a new start, so Nathan and I decided to leave our old life in California and move to Arkansas. I thought that a new husband, a new granddaughter, and a new house would satisfy the restlessness in my heart.

Melissa's boyfriend, Ryan, came around regularly to visit his baby and made up his mind that he wanted to marry Melissa and establish a family. They got married in a real church, actually a Pentecostal church, and for the first time in my life I met true, born-again, Spirit-filled Christians. In fact, the church was full of them! I thought they were all very weird and my philosophies certainly didn't mesh with theirs. But the kids were married and I was a happy mom. Maybe now Melissa would have some stability in her life.

Shortly after she got married, Melissa did more than gain stability—she got saved! That totally freaked me out but the change in her was even more startling. I watched a magnificent metamorphosis take place in my daughter's life and it was wonderful.

Melissa must have started praying for me, because I consented to go to church with her and listen to her pastor. After three visits, I started to understand the plan of salvation and when it finally hit me, I literally *ran* to the altar to accept Jesus.

Because of my past life, I was in bondage to many demons. When the Savior embraced me with His love, I was filled with indescribable joy and hope, although I knew I needed counsel and guidance. I went to a prayer meeting and told some of the women who were praying with me that I felt something still standing between me and Jesus. They began to pray for me, and much to my surprise a voice screamed out of me (not my own voice) and I was thrown to the floor. These women knew they were dealing with spirits and they cast out the demons in the name of Jesus.

It felt like scales had fallen from my eyes; the world was bright and sweet and new, so unlike the hell I had been living in for over thirty years. I began to study the Bible and I received the baptism in the Holy Spirit. Then, best of all, my other children accepted Jesus as Savior.

It has been sixteen years since I got saved, and I have put forth my best effort to follow the Lord and live a righteous, pleasing life. However, there is still one sad aspect of my life, because my husband has not yet come to the Lord. I feel that his painful childhood has made him put up walls, even against the love of God. There are things about my husband that are hard to deal with and he attempts to impede my walk with the Lord. I am learning a new level of trust in God, however, and the children and I know that we will one day have the joy of seeing him become a believer! The Lord gives enough grace to be "more than a conqueror" in all the circumstances of my life.

## Has God Forgotten Us?

I was born into a pastor's family in 1939 and because we were so poor, my mother ate very little during her pregnancy. I was born malnourished, which caused rickets (a nutritional deficiency disease of childhood that affects the bones and causes deformity) and didn't walk until I was three. When I was ten, I contracted polio and had problems in my legs for the rest of my life.

My husband, James, was a chemical engineer with a major company when he felt God's call to the ministry. He began to attend seminary the year we were married, 1960. After a few years, I was able to have one child, a son, and then I was diagnosed with MS (multiple sclerosis). James and I were in a denomination that does not believe in healing or the baptism in the Holy Spirit, but we were serving the Lord in every way possible.

My sister and her husband visited us and invited us to their hometown to attend a seminar being conducted by a renowned, Spirit-filled teacher. They were newly filled with the Holy Spirit and were eager for us to share the experience. We were reluctant to go because of our background, but we were desperate to know more—and they paid for our tickets.

By this time, MS had caused my hands to turn inward and I was beginning to have tremors. My poor troubled legs were becoming even more troubled. At the seminar, I went forward for prayer and the power of God was so strong on me that I fell down. I was semi-conscious all night but was able to realize that the Lord had healed me. My hands had become uncurled and my crooked spine was made straight—in fact, I "grew" two inches!

James and I were baptized in the Holy Spirit and this caused a great controversy. His ordination was revoked and we were asked to leave our church. We were able to connect with a strong man of God about 50 miles from where we lived who helped reestablish us in many ways. We started a charismatic church and did our best to stay right on track with the Word of God. One church in town was very legalistic and dogmatic and did not believe in doctors, wearing glasses, and lots of other common medical remedies. Our congregation was small and we were young, but we knew enough to try to avoid controversy.

After my healing, God blessed us with our second son. Once again our lives were altered in a dramatic way. Our son, Ethan, almost didn't survive (nor did I) and later we found that he had a learning disability. The years of getting him through school were difficult, but he graduated with pride.

He was anointed by the Lord to play the saxophone and he can play anything he hears—it is a precious gift.

Our older son, Jonathan, had a dream of becoming a Spirit-filled surgeon but halfway through college, a girl got his attention and pulled him off track. He never finished medical school and walked away from the Lord and his upbringing. We continued to pray for him (you *never* quit praying for your children) and just this year he is showing signs of change.

God called us to a southern state to live in the midst of horrendous bigotry and greed. We fasted and prayed and taught the people, but we didn't feel like we were getting anyplace. Several times we tried to leave, but the Lord closed the door. We felt that He was telling us to "stay and fight."

James was battling diabetes and it looked like his leg would have to be amputated. God sent along a Jewish doctor who said, "I can save his leg; I know I can." I asked if I could pray over him before surgery and he assented. We could not know at the time that James would have to have seven surgeries, resulting in five months in the hospital and a full year of recuperation. And before each operation I would pray with this dear surgeon.

My mother-in-law had Parkinson's disease and had to have heart surgery during this time, so I was running back and forth trying to take care of everyone. I got so exhausted at times that I thought I was going to collapse. I prayed and sometimes even *begged* the Lord to heal James. His leg wouldn't always heal quickly after surgery. After one surgery, a precious nurse returned from Israel with water from the Jordan River and she poured this on the open wound. James began to improve from that moment.

James never complained in the hospital and his faith never wavered. We have continued to have setbacks but we know we are in God's care. A couple of years ago I was stricken with a deadly blood clot and once again Jesus spared my life.

We often had financial struggles because we were unable to work, and the Lord encouraged us by providing for us from unexpected sources. We praise God for His children who have compassion and reach out to help others. In our case, we felt this was God's way of telling us that He hadn't forgotten us. We received one generous check and I was so overwhelmed with joy and gratitude that I held it to my heart while I took a nap!

When James was in the hospital, the Lord told him, "You have not fulfilled your destiny." The Lord continues to give us strength and we try to touch anyone we can, anyone the Lord sends our way. We know the Lord is still our Healer and we look forward to serving Him many more years.

## ...The Land Allotted to the Righteous

A few years ago my husband and I were in our early thirties with two children, four-and-a-half and three years of age. We had been able to purchase a little home, and our life was what could be considered normal. I planned to home school the boys and, in fact, had already begun activities of that type with them. Except for excruciating headaches that almost incapacitated me at times, everything was going very well for us.

It's interesting how quickly your life can change and while the change may not be dramatic, it can have a profound effect on one's walk with the Lord. Our family life was thrown into a sort of disarray when my husband, Jesse, had to begin traveling. His job kept him out of town for long stretches of time, and I wasn't equipped to handle all that fell on my shoulders.

Besides home schooling, I had to do all the household chores, both inside and outside, or leave them undone and wait for Jesse to do them when he got home. It seems a small thing, but I had to mow the grass (that couldn't always wait for Jesse), and being outdoors in the heat would cause my sinuses to react—causing the horrible headaches. This would have a domino effect because when I had a headache I couldn't care for the boys like I needed to, and so it went. I was accustomed to "running a tight ship" and it bothered me that our life wasn't orderly.

Many times as I walked back and forth in the yard mowing the lawn, I cried and prayed. I shared my heart with God and sometimes just groaned, like it says in the Scriptures. I needed help or healing or change—I certainly needed *something*. And I told God about it.

Even though our house was small, we loved it. It was the first house Jesse and I had purchased together and we had been there only a couple of years. But as he and I talked about our options, we considered looking for a townhouse, where there would not be so much outside work. Surely that would solve some of our problems. We were excited about it until we started looking at them. Our hopes came crashing down when we saw how expensive they were, and how small! Even smaller than our little house. We felt like we were right back at ground zero. What did God want us to do?

We continued to pray and ask God for wisdom. Months passed and as we shared a bit of our struggle with my parents, my dad asked, "Have you ever considered an older townhouse?" No, we hadn't. He told us of some that were older and larger, and in our price range. We got so excited that we went driving through that neighborhood late at night, anxious to see some of the places.

Jesse and I had been seeking God about moving, and the peace He gave us was so amazing. We got a realtor and had such hope and excitement—until we saw the first place. It was absolutely awful and needed a lot of work. With Jesse gone so much, there was no way we could fix up a place. I had the two boys to care for and chronic headaches and...well, we just couldn't consider it. Maybe townhouse number two would be better. But it wasn't.

By now I was starting to get discouraged. Had we missed God? I was trying to remain hopeful, but it was hard when townhouse number three was no better than the other two. We had been so sure of His guidance. Where had we gone wrong? Should we keep looking?

All the questions vanished when we walked into townhouse number four. We were home! There was no denying that this was the place God had in mind for us. It was absolutely perfect; the only thing it lacked was a fireplace, and we could live without a fireplace. "Oh, God, this is it! Please let us get this one." We were encouraged and convinced that we hadn't missed God's will and leading.

We were so excited that we had our families over to see the place. Then we placed a bid on it, but the sellers wouldn't consider it until our house sold. So we listed our house with a realtor and prayed specifically that God would send a buyer right away. I also prayed that our buyers would be people who would love the house as much as we did.

God cares about every aspect of our lives—yes, even the house we buy. Three weeks after we listed our house, we had a buyer. We could now formally bid on the townhouse—and they accepted our bid. Everything was finally running smoothly. Then our realtor called! The sellers had another buyer who would pay full price—and cash. Our realtor was upset, anxious, and obviously stressed out.

Looking back through my journal during those days, I find: "God, help! I am so confused, or tired, or ready to cry!" I included the verse that day that was in the World Challenge Promise Booklet, "For whoever would draw near to God must believe that He exists and that He rewards those who seek Him." (Hebrews 11:6) This had always been one of my favorite verses and here it was when I was feeling so low. How His Word encouraged my heart.

It was Easter weekend and we were tempted to take on the worries of our realtor, but I knew deep down that God was in control. We trusted Him to work things out, and we refused to take on this burden. Since it was a holiday, there was nothing we could do, anyway. Well, that's not quite true, because we could go to God.

> "As the mountains are round about Jerusalem, so the Lord is round about His people, from this time forth and for evermore. For the scepter of wickedness shall not rest upon the land allotted to the righteous...." (Psalm 125:2,3)

Through these precious words, God assured me that the townhouse was ours. No matter what the circumstances looked like, no matter what our realtor thought, God was keeping it for us, His righteous ones—righteous because of Jesus Christ our Savior. I had a peace that passes all understanding, indeed.

Here's the good news: The sellers did not accept the other offer of more money in cash. Their refusal makes no sense, but that's what they did. God turns the hearts of kings and He can sway decisions people make. He worked a miracle for us and showed us His tender love.

The blessings just continue! Let me list a few of them:

- God led me to doctors who performed surgery that helped alleviate my headaches.
- My husband is traveling much less than before.
- I am now in my sixth year of home schooling and things are going well.
- And almost all the yard work is done by our association!

God answered everything in His time and in His way, and He showed me that He is in control. Truly I am His daughter and He loves me and cares about my needs and desires.

## Never, Never, *Never* Give Up

This testimony will be short, but I want to encourage those of you who are praying for unsaved loved ones and aren't seeing any visible results.

My husband was of the Mormon faith and there was constant tension and conflict in our home over "religion" and related matters. I struggled to keep the arguing to a minimum but many times through the years I told the Lord I didn't see how I could go on. I tried to live peaceably and glorify the Lord with my life so that I would be a good witness to our three daughters. They all eventually accepted Jesus into their hearts and are serving Him.

I have a real miracle testimony! After 48 years of praying for my husband, he recently accepted our precious Lord Jesus into his heart. I had prayed for years that he would allow me to tithe, and two weeks ago he told me to start tithing. Praise God—I now feel like a "legal" Christian! The change in my husband is just breathtaking and I am filled with a new joy!

My mother-in-law had always loved me but for 46 years she had fought me over Jesus—she just didn't want to hear me talk about Him. When she was 86 years old, I once again told her that I wanted her to know my Jesus. I asked her if she would like to ask Him into her heart, and this time she said, "Yes." This dear, sweet Mormon woman prayed the prayer of salvation with me, and two years later she was walking with Jesus in heaven.

I just want to encourage others to persevere in prayer for their loved ones. It isn't always easy, but if we press on and stay faithful, we will see victory! My heart is overwhelmed when I think about the awesome love, mercy, and victory that is ours in Christ.